THE
MAKING OF AMERICA
SERIES

LAKE MARTIN
ALABAMA'S CROWN JEWEL

THIS WORK IS DEDICATED TO THE ANGELS OF CHILDREN'S HARBOR.

IN MEMORY OF MINTON ROLLO ALLEN (1925–2002)

TRAM ROSE FERRY. This unique railed ferry transported a railroad engine across the Tallapoosa River in Elmore County in 1898.

THE
MAKING OF AMERICA
SERIES

LAKE MARTIN
ALABAMA'S CROWN JEWEL

ELIZABETH D. SCHAFER

ARCADIA

Published by Arcadia Publishing,
an imprint of Tempus Publishing, Inc.
2 Cumberland Street
Charleston, SC 29401

Printed in Great Britain.

Library of Congress Catalog Card Number: 2002107474

For all general information contact Arcadia Publishing at:
Telephone 843-853-2070
Fax 843-853-0044
E-Mail sales@arcadiapublishing.com

For customer service and orders:
Toll-Free 1-888-313-2665

Visit us on the Internet at http://www.arcadiapublishing.com

FRONT COVER: *The Alabama Power Company Overlook provides a panoramic view of Lake Martin. Viewers can see Kowaliga Bay, Kowaliga Creek Highway Bridge, Children's Harbor, islands, and a variety of watercraft.*

4

Contents

ACKNOWLEDGMENTS

With gratitude to my parents Carolyn and Robert Schafer; Sean Fitzgerald Allen; Ethel Allen; Charles D. McCrary, president, and Bill Tharpe, archivist, of the Alabama Power Company Corporate Archives; Ben and Luanne Russell; Bobbie and Jim Parkinson; Luttrell Lord; Marilyn Cooper; Jean and Henry Henderson; Dean Hays-Elam; Beverly Webster; John Robertson; Marilyn Ray; Dana Rickman; Mary Lee Carter; Jerry Meadows and Dr. Frank L. Owsley Jr., who taught me Alabama history; Dwayne Cox, Joyce Hicks, Chris Mixon, Brenda Ray, Andrew Adams, Brenda Prather, and John Varner at the Auburn University library; Susie Anderson, Regina Strickland, and Dana Franklin at the Horseshoe Bend Regional Library, Dadeville, Alabama; Cynthia Luckie and Mary Jo Madison Scott at the Alabama Department of Archives and History; James L. Noles Jr. and Harvey H. Jackson III for their fabulous histories of the Alabama Power Company and Tallapoosa River; Kathryn Holland Braund for her insightful Creek and Bartram scholarship; the late Dorothy Jean (Deeje) Nichols Mitchell Justice; Roberta Haden Greene; Connie Browning; Kim Appel; John Phillips; Charles Farrow; Marquita Campbell; Blue Vardeman; Jim and Debbie Bain and all the people who have contributed to creating *Lake Martin Living*; the Hollins University English Department; in memory of High Voltage Nickie; and kháwp khun khâ to Kuhn Somsak, Wirote, Nuaprang, Yaowarat, Thitima, Laksanee, Ekaraj, Archakorn, Pipob, Fon, Santi, Chaiyut, Kate, Bird, Methee, Phaikrit, Preamporn, Ekchai, and Dr. Sawitree and friends, who made Rayong and Bangkok, Thailand, half the world away from Lake Martin, a second home. Perhaps some day Loy Krathong, the Thai water festival, can be celebrated at Lake Martin.

1. EBB AND FLOW

Lake Martin, created in the remote southeastern Alabama wilderness in 1926, has become one of the state's most prized recreational treasures. Originally called Cherokee Bluffs Lake and often referred to as Alabama's crown jewel, Lake Martin has attracted generations of people to enjoy its tranquil waters. As a home, vacation spot, or competition site, scenic Lake Martin offers a variety of possibilities to fulfill people's recreational desires. From enhancing pleasure boating, sailing, and water skiing to hosting family reunions, bass fishing tournaments, and peaceful weekend retreats, Lake Martin is a magical utopia. The lake's soothing clear water sparkles and laps reassuringly against its shores, rejuvenating tired spirits and bodies. Lake Martin's grandeur and serene scenery are stunning.

Located on the Piedmont plateau near the tip of the southern Appalachian foothills, Lake Martin dominates Tallapoosa County and dips into northeastern Elmore and southeastern Coosa Counties. At Cherokee Bluffs, Martin Dam contains the Tallapoosa River and several of its tributaries to form the lake as an impounded reservoir of storage water to generate hydroelectric power for Alabama and the southeast. The freshwater lake also provides flood control and ensures that the Alabama River, which is formed by the joining of the Tallapoosa and Coosa Rivers at Wetumpka, is navigable to the Gulf Coast.

The lake is the namesake of Thomas Wesley Martin, who identified Cherokee Bluffs as the most suitable dam and reservoir site. While Martin was president of the Alabama Power Company from 1920 to 1949, he oversaw the creation of Lake Martin and pioneered a hydroelectric power system that transformed Alabama and the South. Martin also monitored construction of two other Tallapoosa River dams, Thurlow and Yates, below Martin Dam. Lake Martin contributed to the Alabama Power Company's ability to offer rural transmissions and provide surplus power to other states.

Lake Martin's level fluctuates based on the power company's energy needs. Usually, the power company drops the lake's level about 10 feet every fall and winter. After the water has receded from shorelines, people can repair docks and seawalls. When the dam's gates open, nearby residents can feel the earth shake.

Hydrological authorities declared Lake Martin the world's largest artificial lake when it was created. The 31-mile-long, man-made lake's water covers approximately 44,000 acres and has 750 miles of shoreline. When Lake Martin formed in 1926, it was larger than the

MARTIN DAM AND LAKE MARTIN. From this site, impounded water stretches back 31 miles.

area of Birmingham. The deepest sections of the lake were 180 feet from the bottom to the surface. Lake Martin's unique shape, resembling the outline of a dragon, is due to how dammed water fills the river's twisting tributaries.

Lake Martin is an isolated paradise yet is conveniently near cities that played significant roles in its creation. Auburn is only 26 miles away. Montgomery is approximately 50 miles to the southwest, and Birmingham is 75 miles to the northwest. Atlanta, Georgia is 130 miles to the northeast. The Gulf Coast is a three-and-one-half-hour drive from the lake.

The Tallapoosa River and its tributaries attracted people, from Native Americans to migrants from eastern states, to settle an area that was later transformed into Lake Martin. Lake Martin became a community for modern residents of east-central Alabama, who call it home, in addition to people from across the United States and foreign countries, who often return annually to visit favorite places and reunite with friends and family. People enjoy exploring the lake's many sloughs, islands, and coves.

Lake Martin has a subtropical climate, averaging 60 inches of rain annually. The hot, humid weather is characterized by afternoon thunderstorms. The Lake Martin area is appealing to natives and snowbirds because of its mild temperatures that rarely freeze.

Lake Martin's shores are thick with shady pine trees. Pine needles coat the ground and float in the water. White and pink dogwood flowers dot the piney woods. Fish playfully leap from the lake, their splashes echoing through the quiet stillness. Ducks march their ducklings toward lake cabins. Some hummingbirds are so tame that they perch on people's shoulders. Pudgy chameleons bask in the sun. Great blue herons, purple martins, eagles, deer, and snapping turtles thrive in Lake Martin's habitats. Domesticated animals consider Lake Martin home, too. Cats sleep on docks, dogs ride in boats, and horses trod bridle paths.

Lake Martin is a wonderland for water sports. Regattas and water skiing competitions gracefully glide across the lake. Considered one of the best bass-fishing lakes in Alabama and the Southeast, Lake Martin offers year-round fishing opportunities, and numerous fishing tournaments are held there. Anglers can hire fishing guides to direct them to places that the biggest fish might lurk. Fishermen develop strategies, figuring which lures might attract prize fish. Record catches have included a 33-plus-pound striped bass.

Over the decades, Lake Martin has developed a resort atmosphere yet retains a small-town sense of community. The friendly lake lifestyle includes everyone. Area publications, especially *Lake Martin Living*, reflect people's love for and dedication to Lake Martin. Lake people generously help each other repair boats and docks and share recipes and equipment. Laughter and humor are abundant. Boat parades show creativity as people decorate boats in holiday or patriotic themes and wear costumes.

A natural playground for all ages, Lake Martin has nurtured generations of lake enthusiasts. Grandparents teach grandchildren how to swim, boat, and fish in the same waters where they learned those skills several decades prior. Lake Martin is also therapeutic, bringing faith, joy, dignity, and a sense of independence to people dealing with serious illnesses or physical disabilities at such sanctuaries as Children's Harbor and Camp ASCCA (Alabama Special Camp for Children and Adults).

National publications have named Lake Martin the best American retirement spot. Investment opportunities abound. Lake Martin has benefited the region's economy by creating jobs and generating revenue.

Many famous people have lived at or visited Lake Martin. Throughout the decades since the lake was created, regional and national celebrities and political leaders have considered Lake Martin a retreat where they can relax and enjoy the fellowship of sport and nature. Governors, including George and Lurleen Wallace, Frank M. Dixon, William W. Brandon, and Gordon Persons, have spoken at ceremonies, relaxed in cabins, or skied across the lake. Football players, such as Bo Jackson and Joe Namath, have fished here.

PONTOON BOATS ON LAKE MARTIN. Boaters often gather at beautiful Chimney Rock to fish, visit, and relax.

Local lore often reminisces about how the legendary Hank Williams Sr. wrote classic country songs, including "Kaw-Liga," when he was inspired by Lake Martin's mythical past.

The area's unique culture reveals people's mutual love for the lake, expressed by universally known traditions and names such as Goat Island, Kowaliga, and teenagers daring each other to jump from the heights of Chimney Rock. Legends, tall tales, and ghost stories reflect the history of the Lake Martin area and its mysteries, including rumors of hidden treasure and gold lost underneath the deepest water. The lake water covered Native American artifacts and hid long-forgotten secrets. Beloved communities like Susanna exist only in memories and in ghost towns beneath Lake Martin's surface where boats and skiers glide.

Lake Martin inspires reminiscences of adventures, friendships, and the fish that got away. Everyone has their own Lake Martin stories, and libraries could be filled with millions of Lake Martin tales. This book will share some of my favorite stories about lake-related people, places, and events that will introduce newcomers to the lake's heritage while reminding locals how their contributions have made Lake Martin a prized place.

SUNSET AT CHEROKEE BLUFFS. This artist's painting was featured on the cover of the September 1923 Powergrams.

2. NATIVES, EXPLORERS, AND WARRIORS

The Lake Martin area witnessed amazing events long before the lake was formed. Much of the region's prehistory is uncertain, although its geological record hints about what the ancient lake site might have been like. At one time, the Gulf Coast was located farther north, lapping at a shore in central Alabama near Tallassee. Geologists have found evidence of both sea and terrestrial dinosaurs in Alabama. Although no fossilized dinosaur remains have been located at Lake Martin, it is possible that dinosaurs might have lived in the area.

An ancient asteroid struck central Alabama. In July 1998, geologists drilled at the 4.5-mile crater site near Wetumpka looking for "shocked quartz" because that mineral is created by intense pressure and heat equivalent to an asteroid crash. The impact of the asteroid would have rocked the area that later would become Lake Martin. Auburn University geologist David King hypothesized that a football stadium–sized asteroid was moving 12 miles per second before it hit Earth with 30 times more force than any known nuclear bomb detonations.

Archeological evidence indicates that ancient people once lived in central Alabama. The Stone Age Indians left artifacts that provide clues about their lives. More information about life centuries later in the Lake Martin area is known for certain, although precise details are questionable. For example, in September 1540, Spanish explorer Hernando de Soto and his men probably marched across land that is now beneath Lake Martin. This expedition had been organized in 1537 after Holy Roman Emperor Charles V granted de Soto permission to search for gold in the New World. Rumors of a wealthy wilderness empire with magnificent treasures intrigued the men. At that time, Spain owned the area that later became western Florida and southern Alabama.

De Soto and 1,000 adventurers sailed across the Atlantic Ocean and reached the west Florida coast (near modern St. Petersburg) in 1539. They were welcomed in New Spain where they prepared for their explorations. For three years, the conquistadors trekked through the southeast, covering an average of 5 to 6 leagues (approximately 13 to 16 miles) per day. Records of their journey documented their passage through Native American communities near the Tallapoosa River. Scholars have debated the exact route of the de Soto explorers through east-central Alabama.

Armed with shields, crossbows, and lances, the men marched on horseback south from Toasi (Talladega) for five days. Their path probably would have crossed lands now submerged underneath Lake Martin. Some modern writers speculated that de Soto might

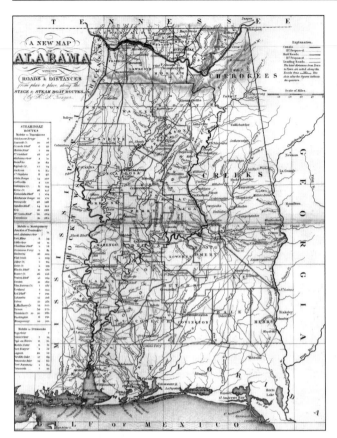

"A New Map of Alabama," 1833. H.S. Tanner's map shows Native American names for places that later were submerged beneath Lake Martin.

have camped near modern Eclectic in August 1540. As they moved through Alabama, advance scouts brought information about where to trek. By day, they wandered on trails through the thicketed woodlands, frequently encountering wildlife and occasionally meeting Native Americans. At villages, the Spaniards sometimes participated in such festivities as feasts, horse racing, and ball games. On several nights, a full moon shone over their camp. The conquistadors followed the Tallapoosa River, crossing it with rafts and canoes.

A sixteenth-century account of de Soto's journey described Tallise as a large town located on the bend of a deep river. Some accounts place this Creek village near modern Childersburg where the modern De Soto Caverns are located instead of Tallassee. De Soto and his men spent one night at Tallise before heading westward to Caxa (near modern Wetumpka) on the Coosa River. Their further travels resulted in battle against Native Americans at Maubila.

After leaving Alabama, de Soto's group headed west, reaching and crossing the Mississippi River in 1541, then seeking treasure in parts of modern Arkansas, Oklahoma, and Texas. Disappointed by not finding riches, de Soto ordered his company to return east. He died from a fever, and his men sunk his body in the Mississippi River to prevent Native American enemies from destroying his corpse. Some survivors returned to the Gulf of Mexico where Spanish military fortifications and communities had been established.

For centuries, Native American tribes lived, hunted, traded, and raised families on the land that is now submerged underneath Lake Martin or adjacent to its shores. Cherokee, Alibamos, Choctaw, Chickasaw, and especially Muskogee (also spelled Muscogulge), usually called Creek, Native Americans depended on the Tallapoosa River and its tributaries for both food and mobility.

The Creek Nation was the southeast's largest Native American community, consisting of allied tribes. Creeks lived in Alabama, Georgia, and Florida. Tribes established significant towns such as the Upper Creek settlement Kialiga along the Tallapoosa River. The Tallapoosas were an ethnic group of Creeks who lived in the Upper towns' geopolitical division. Linguists, historians, and anthropologists disagree about the source of the name Tallapoosa, although its Native American origins are not disputed. Many people believe that the river's name was derived from the Choctaw words "tali" and "pushi," meaning "pulverized rock."

The Creeks were a spiritual people who believed that the creator gave their ancestors land that must be carefully tended and protected. To them, land was not a material possession but a spiritual essence that it was the Creeks' responsibility to nurture and respect. The Creeks valued the crops and wildlife that thrived on the land. Produce and animals were carefully cultivated and hunted to sell to Chickasaw, Choctaw, and Cherokee tribes and European traders. At the summer holiday Busk, also

TUKABAHCHI HISTORICAL MARKER. People have referred to this town as the Manhattan of the Creek Nation.

known as the Green Corn Dance, the Creek sacrificed part of their crop in hopes of being rewarded with ample harvests.

Okfuskee was the Creek Confederacy's largest settlement, and Tukabatchee (also spelled Tukabahchi), which was located near modern Tallassee in Elmore County, was the Upper Creek Nation's capital. Archaeological excavations of this and other sites revealed information about the area's early settlers. A Creek village was located by Kowaliga Creek (sometimes spelled Kialiga or Kealedji among many variations) until 1836. The Kowaliga tribe lived in an area that is under the modern lake. An 1832 census recorded 591 Indians and two black slaves. Chiefs Quas-Lad-Harjo and Doak-Car-Micco led the Creeks, while the Harjo, Yoholo, Fixico, and Emarthlar families dominated Kowaliga. In villages, visitor Caleb Swan observed that log "houses stand in clusters of four, five, six, seven and eight together, irregularly distributed up and down the banks of rivers or small streams." Kowaliga also had a teokofa, or hot house, for ceremonial cleansings.

The Tallapoosa River Creeks lived according to traditions and social systems, including established kinship and inheritance patterns, established by previous generations. Creek families consisted of a man and woman and their children. Usually women chose their husbands subject to clan elders approval. Elders sometimes recommended marital partners, and both people had to agree to the marriage. Female representatives of the bride and groom discussed the proposal and evidence that the groom could materially provide for his wife. Acceptance of gifts such as clothing and blankets represented acceptance. The

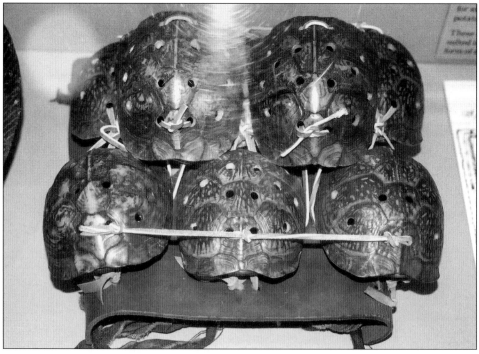

TORTOISE SHELL LEG RATTLES. *These rattles were worn by the Creeks. Turtles thrived in the Tallapoosa River and its tributaries.*

*DIAGRAM OF
KOWALIGA TOWN.
Julius Frank of the
Alabama
Anthropological Society
drew this plan of the
town's square ground.*

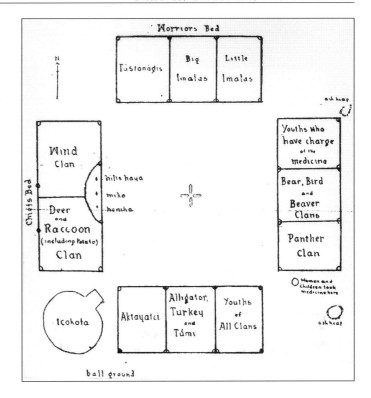

marriage ceremony involved the groom building a house, planting and harvesting a crop, hunting for meat, and presenting these items to his bride. The Creeks then considered her bound to him.

Creeks were affiliated with clans according to their maternal lineage, and clans designated an Indian's social status. Married couples belonged to different clans. Children and mothers shared the same matrilineage that comprised the main family unit. Clans were often identified by animal totems, such as an eagle, which symbolized the qualities associated with the ancestress. Creeks' lives were directed by their clans, which assigned land for crops and determined punishments for wrongdoers. The elders also prepared males for leadership roles within clans.

Female Creeks lived near members of their clans. Husbands moved to their wife's village and performed construction and agricultural tasks, but did not own those family properties and produce. Extended families shared dwellings and daily chores and activities. Women of all ages and relationships were supportive of each other. Boys tended to have closer relationships with maternal uncles or esteemed clan elders than with their fathers.

The seasons, gender roles, and traditions regulated Creeks' lives. Women and men often functioned separately within their communities. "Every family has two huts or cabins," an American military officer noted about a Creek village. He commented about Creek family dwellings that "one is the man's, and the other belongs to his wife, where she stays and does her work, seldom or ever coming into the man's house, unless to bring him victuals, or on other errands." Despite separations, Creek males and females sustained romantic relationships and cooperated to nurture their families.

Fishing and hunting were primarily jobs for men. Creeks caught fish with nets, baskets, bows and arrows, and occasionally plants that could be used to drug fish. Men hunted deer, turkey, beaver, wolves, and sometimes bears to provide food for their family and to collect deerskins and pelts. Usually, hunting was the Creeks' primary focus from October through late winter so that the remainder of the year could be devoted to cultivating agricultural crops. Women frequently traveled with their husbands on extended winter hunts conducted away from their village so that they could process hides and preserve meat. Creek families lived in winter hunting camps on ranges associated with the men's clans, while their home villages appeared deserted except for those Creeks who could not travel. In addition to performing routine household chores, women scraped, soaked, stretched, tanned, smoked, and dyed hides to produce the supple skins that European traders preferred.

During most of the year at home, each extended family had land within their village's communal cornfield. Men were expected to maintain this agricultural site, planting and harvesting corn, Creeks' primary nutritional source, for their wife's family. They were also responsible for erecting necessary buildings for public meetings and ceremonies in addition to dwellings and structures to store corn and tools. Men carved pines from the Tallapoosa River area into canoes and pipes. Creeks ground rocks into implements, weapons, and toys.

Male Creeks waged war only to protect their village against invaders or to avenge assaults on honor and character of both living and deceased clan members. Every day, Creek males met in cabins at the public square to talk about issues relevant to their community and the greater Creek Nation. Village government was shaped by group approval of policies. Although women were not permitted at these meetings, they influenced their husbands and male relatives, particularly in matters related to waging war and the treatment of captured enemies.

Creek women focused on domestic concerns at home. They tended to the needs of their children and extended family. Women were responsible for all aspects of food preparation. After men planted the communal cornfield, women and children removed insects from stalks and cobs and weeded their family's plots. Women also grew vegetables in gardens by their homes and gathered berries, nuts, and honey. Roots provided starches for cooking. They processed and preserved foodstuffs with various techniques such as smoking, sun-drying, parching, and grinding. Women were responsible for ensuring their families had ample supplies of drinking water. They also dipped water from area streams and the river to use for cooking and picked up pine branches to build cooking fires. Tallapoosa River Creeks would have eaten meals consisting of venison, fish, squirrel, or rabbit supplemented with hominy, cornmeal, fruits, or vegetables.

Tallapoosa River Creek women were constantly active. In addition to securing cooking water and wood, they toted those supplies for other uses. Creek women's duties also included medical care. Indian women roamed the Tallapoosa River woods to find plants known for their healing tendencies. They stripped bark and leaves from trees and shrubs and dug up roots. Women searched for feathers and animal fur, weaving blankets and clothing from readily available opossum and rabbit hair. They used plants, particularly grasses and river reeds, to make baskets. Clays and mud from the Tallapoosa River and creek banks were used to mold pottery.

Creek women also processed deerskins and furs their male relatives brought home from hunts and transformed them into clothes, shoes, and necessary items. Tallapoosa River Creeks wore deerskins that were called brain tan because they were tanned with a process involving application of brains and smoke. Deerskin moccasins, shirts, and breeches were durable and weather-resistant. Women often made clothing into elaborate costumes and also created decorative handicrafts. Creek women wore deerskin skirts and jackets, sometimes trimmed with beads, lace, and embroidery. They braided their long hair and occasionally tattooed their skin. Historians are unsure who Creek Beloved Women were in Creek society, although the title suggests that they were revered, wise women who probably significantly impacted their communities.

Creek men often ritually purified themselves prior to hunts, ceremonies, ball games, or battles by secluding themselves from female contact. Creek women were often isolated from men during their menstrual cycles and childbirth to maintain purity standards essential for Creek ceremonies. An observer noted that Creek men "oblige their women in their lunar retreats, to build small huts,at as considerable a distance from their dwelling-houses, as they imagine may be out of the enemies reach." He emphasized that "during the space of that period, they are obliged to stay at the risqué [*sic*] of their lives. Should they be known to violate that ancient law, they must answer for every misfortune that befalls any of the people."

Plan of an ancient *chunkey* yard, 1789. *Chunkey* was played with a smooth stone and wooden poles. The object was to throw the pole as close to the *chunkey* stone as possible.

CHUNKEY FIELD DESIGN. Creek men competed to see who had the best spear-throwing skills.

HORSESHOE BEND IN THE TALLAPOOSA RIVER. The Creeks refer to this area in the curve of the river as Tohopeka.

Creek recreation varied, and leisure activities were pursued for both entertainment and practical reasons. Men played vigorous ball games with sticks and deerskin balls to condition their bodies and hone their reflexes for war. Chunkey was a pastime in which men threw spears at a rolling stone in an attempt to hit the ground nearest where the stone stopped. Creeks played musical instruments, especially wooden flutes.

Creeks hunted white-tailed deer not only as a source of meat, but also to tan skins for trade. Deerskins, the most significant trading item for Creeks, were especially sought by European traders who exported them to England and the continent. The abundant Tallapoosa River ecosystem wildlife assured economic security for area Native Americans. Creeks used furs to establish alliances with Europeans and secure reliable sources of desired European goods, especially wool, leather, luxury items like mirrors, manufactured textiles, tools, agricultural implements, sewing equipment, and weapons of a quality that the Creeks could not technologically produce. Gradually, the Creeks became reliant on these imported goods. They began to hunt and trap with commercial motivations instead of solely for self and tribal subsistence. European influences gradually altered Creek customs and culture.

During the eighteenth century, European explorers and traders interacted with Tallapoosa River Indians. In 1735, British soldiers and Georgia Rangers built Fort Okfuskee near the site of the modern Martin Dam. The British hoped to secure control of trade with the Creeks at that extensive village, but were unsuccessful in convincing the

Creeks to trade exclusively with them instead of with the French. They attempted to prevent French spies and forces from nearby Fort Toulouse at the junction of the Alabama and Coosa Rivers from encroaching on territory the British desired.

When traders visited Creek towns during the eighteenth century, the village headman encouraged a trader to marry a Creek woman, preferably one of his relatives. The Creeks approved of such marriages to secure stable trading alliances. Creek wives were useful to white traders as interpreters of Creek languages. They explained Creek customs to their husbands and warned them of taboos and dangers. Their families protected the traders' property and merchandise. Creeks accepted mixed-blood children. Most Tallapoosa River Creek mothers insisted that their brothers or uncles teach their sons about Creek ceremonial and political practices and cultural heritage. Sometime trader husbands convinced Creek wives to send sons to cities for education.

Traveling through Alabama, naturalist William visited Native American villages and described them accurately. He countered European stereotypes about Creeks and Cherokees and described them as industrious people with strong family systems. "The Muscogulge women, though remarkably short of stature, are well formed," he said, describing "their visage round, features regular and beautiful; the brow high and arched; the eye large, black, and languishing, expressive of modesty, diffidence, and bashfulness." Bartram considered the Creeks to be "loving and affectionate."

In 1790, the United States government and the Creeks signed the Treaty of New York to initiate the "Civilization Program" in an attempt to transform the Creek economy. The government gave Creeks livestock and iron plows hoping that the Creeks would choose to farm instead of hunt commercially. If they did, the government could more easily

CANNON USED AT THE BATTLE OF HORSESHOE BEND. This weapon gave the United States troops a miliary advantage over the Creeks.

acquire the Creeks' hunting lands. Creek women received spinning wheels and looms. The government initiated a program to teach Creeks white etiquette methods. A secret treaty article stated the federal government would "educate and clothe such of the Creek youth as shall be agreed upon, not exceeding four in number at any one time." By 1796, federal Creek representative Benjamin Hawkins monitored the progress of the program and noted that some private Creek farms were raising cattle and cotton. The program failed, though, because it was contrary to the communal and matrilineal character and gender roles of the Creek clans.

Near modern Lake Martin, a Tallapoosa River bend shaped like a horseshoe was the site of a significant War of 1812 battle. From 1812 to 1815, the United States and Great Britain disagreed about the neutral powers' maritime rights. The United States was particularly angered that the British Royal Navy had impressed American seamen. Several years before, in 1807, the British had also captured and executed crewmen from the U.S.S. *Chesapeake* in American territorial waters. Both Great Britain and France had approved blockades and confiscation of American ships and cargoes. Despite economic efforts, such as temporarily ceasing trade with the British, the United States was ineffective at convincing Great Britain to respect United States neutrality. On June 18, 1812, the United States Congress decided to declare war against Great Britain. At first, troops participated in battles at strategic sites in Canada and around Detroit.

At the same time, the United States faced another foe. In what was considered the southwest United States at that time, angry Creek Indians resented white settlers on the Alabama frontier, which was part of the Mississippi Territory. The Creeks separated into factions. Some Creek leaders, encouraged by agent Benjamin Hawkins, promoted peaceful resolution of the problem of settlers trespassing on Indian lands, while others were eager to wage war. The peaceful Lower Creeks, known as White Sticks, were not militant like the Upper Creeks, called Red Sticks, who painted their war clubs red. The White Sticks were willing to sell some land to whites in the hope of appeasing them.

The Creek War of 1813–1814 pitted Indians against Americans and also Indians against Indians in a civil war. In the northern United States, the Shawnee chief Tecumseh and his brother Tenskwatawa, who was called the Prophet, encouraged all Indians to ally with the British. Tecumseh thought that Native American territory belonged universally to all Indians and could not be transferred to non-Indians from any tribe. He urged Indians to resist white encroachment on tribal lands and hunting grounds. Tecumseh traveled to many Indian villages throughout the wilderness of the United States to rally and unite warriors. He shouted, "Let the white race perish." Tecumseh's dramatic rhetoric escalated Indians' hatred of whites. He described whites as being evil because "They seize your land; they corrupt your women, they trample on the ashes of your dead! Back whence they came, upon a trail of blood, they must be driven." Tecumseh assured Indians that prophets protected Indians from harm with their supernatural powers. A wave of nativist spiritualism encouraged Indians to behave fanatically to destroy whites.

Accounts indicate that Tecumseh visited Tallapoosa River Creeks in autumn 1811 to recruit members for his confederation. Tecumseh felt an affinity for Creeks because his mother was a Tuckabatche Creek and his oldest brother was born in the Tallapoosa River area. Local Indians, however, did not accept his warmongering because they did not feel

WILLIAM WEATHERFORD. Also known as Red Eagle, Chief Weatherford surrendered to Andrew Jackson and sought peaceful resolutions to the American-Creek conflict.

threatened by whites. Most white traders had treated area Creeks with respect and seemed uninterested in securing their ancestral lands.

At one village, Tecumseh, frustrated that area Creek chieftains did not support his ideas, supposedly said:

> You will not march with Tecumseh against the pale-face foes of your fathers. You have become squaws—you who wear the feathers of Warrior chiefs. You call Kowaliga a "red town" but the blood of your fathers has turned to water in your veins.
>
> Very well. Tecumseh will go. Tecumseh goes to Detroit to carry a message—a message that the chiefs of the Upper Creek Nation are squaws parading in war paint.
>
> When Tecumseh reaches Detroit he will stamp his foot and your houses will fall down. And when your houses fall you may know Tecumseh is with his people.

According to legend, a large boulder was imprinted with Tecumseh's footprint. Alabama historian Albert Pickett said that after Tecumseh left, Indians witnessed a comet and "One day a mighty rumbling was heard in the earth; the houses of Tookabatcha reeled and tottered." This earthquake shook the future Lake Martin area, and "the first and only earthquake in the history of this Black Belt country made kindling wood of almost every log home in the Upper Creek Nation." The earthquake convinced Creeks to go to war. Tecumseh's Rock, a local landmark located in a modern lake cabin yard, preserves this aspect of Lake Martin's Indian history.

Friction between Creeks intensified when Chickasaws incorrectly told a group of Creeks in February 1813 that the United States and Creek Nation were already at war. As a result, the Creeks murdered seven white families. After Hawkins insisted the Creeks be punished, a tribal council sentenced them to death. Red Sticks then went on the warpath to slay several of the executioners, commit atrocities, and raze nearby villages where Hawkins's supporters lived. The July 1813 shooting of Creek warriors by whites at Burnt Corn Creek angered the Red Sticks.

Incited to fight, a member of the Creek Wind clan, Chief William Weatherford, known as Lumhe Chatti, which means Red Eagle, ordered his warriors to assault Fort Mims on August 30, 1813. Fort Mims was a stockade in southern Alabama on the Alabama River. Commander Major Daniel Beasley, ignoring slaves' warnings that hostile Indians were nearby, did not close the stockade's gates, and a thousand Red Sticks rushed inside to attack. Despite the settlers' pleas for mercy, the Indians slaughtered approximately 500 people.

The torture and massacre of children and women especially outraged American military leaders. An expansionist who saw the opportunity to secure Creek land, Major General Andrew Jackson demanded "retaliatory vengeance." He warned whites about the dangers posed by Red Sticks, saying "Already do they advance towards your frontier, with their scalping knives unsheathed, to butcher your wives, your children, and your helpless babes." Red Eagle was saddened by the killing of women and children and told his tribes he preferred seeking peaceful ways to resolve land issues with whites.

The whites began building up their military resources. Brigadier General John Coffee, commander of the Tennessee militia, recruited men for two mounted regiments to join his cavalry brigade already preparing for retaliatory action in Alabama. By November 3, 1813, his troops reached Tallushatchee, a Creek village along the Coosa River. The Tennesseans attacked the Creeks who were unprepared for the assault. Only 5 Tennessee soldiers died and 41 were wounded during the fighting in contrast to 183 Creek casualties.

Six days later, the Tennesseans helped Brigadier General William Carroll's troops slay approximately 290 Creeks during the Battle of Talladega before the Indians retreated. Fifteen American soldiers died that day, and 80 were wounded. Jackson ordered that his army secure replacements and supplies before engaging in further military action. The inexperienced troops impeded continued success. On January 22, 1814, the American forces endured the vicious Battle of Emuckfau Creek. Reserve forces failed to support Coffee's troops. Although Carroll's militia rescued the Tennesseans, Coffee suffered a serious wound. During the American withdrawal two days later to get supplies, they were attacked in what is called the Battle of Enotachopco and retreated to Fort Strother by the Coosa River. The Creeks celebrated, claiming victory over "Capt. Jack." They also disdainfully called him "Old Mad Jackson."

CHIEF MENEWA. Menewa was a Red Stick leader who led Creek forces at the Battle of Horseshoe Bend and committed other hostile acts toward American allies.

The American forces convalesced, regrouped, and reconnoitered, preparing to battle the Creeks again. Men became bored. Some militiamen's enlistments expired and troop size dwindled. Jackson executed some men who posed mutiny threats when Jackson insisted they extend their service. The state militias were federalized, and he pressured his men to fight. Carroll's troops were more compliant because he boosted morale without resorting to threats.

Meanwhile, the Creeks were aware that the Americans intended to defeat them and would persevere. Gathered on the land extending in the Tallapoosa River's horseshoe bend, which the Creeks called Tohopeka, War Chief Menewa of Okfuskee and a thousand Red Stick warriors awaited attack. They constructed a log barricade reinforced with mud that stretched 400 yards across the field. Women and children stayed with them in this camp. The Creeks were determined to defend their land.

Nearby, Jackson organized a 3,300-soldier army assembled from United States regulars, members of the Tennessee militia, and allied warriors from Cherokee and Lower Creek tribes friendly to the American cause. Coffee recovered from his battle injury to lead his troops.

The American forces who fought at Horseshoe Bend represented the hardscrabble frontier nature of the South. The Tennessee Volunteers, sometimes called "dirty shirts" because of their rustic frontiersmen characteristics, included teenage brothers Joel and Joe

Walker who had left home for adventures. In contrast, Major General Thomas Pinckney was an American Revolution veteran who had served in the United States Congress, as South Carolina governor, and had been the United States minister to Great Britain prior to fighting at Horseshoe Bend. Some of the soldiers became American heroes, including Samuel Houston who was so seriously wounded at Horseshoe Bend that surgeons believed he would die. Contrary to many historical accounts, Davy Crockett did not fight at the Battle of Horseshoe Bend.

William McIntosh commanded friendly Creek soldiers at Horseshoe Bend. Sequoyah, who later created the Cherokee alphabet, served in a cavalry unit at Horseshoe Bend. Previously, Pushmahata had visited villages after Tecumseh in an effort to convince Native Americans not to join Tecumseh's confederation and attack white settlers. His oratory

ANDREW JACKSON. The Red Sticks called him "Old Mad Jackson," but Americans considered him a hero because of his Horseshoe Bend fame, and later elected him president.

convinced his fellow Choctaws to fight with the Americans at Horseshoe Bend. Jackson called Pushmahata the "greatest and bravest Indian I have ever known." Pushmahata later received military rank, uniform, and honors for his support during the Creek War.

Early on March 27, 1814, Jackson ordered his men to initiate a frontal assault while their Indian allies simultaneously swam across the Tallapoosa River to invade from behind to block the Red Sticks from fleeing. Defending their territory, the Red Sticks determinedly fought despite being outnumbered and lacking sufficient weaponry. Initially, soldiers firing the two American cannons were unable to level the barricade. The allied forces attacking the Red Stick camp from the river enabled soldiers to storm the breastworks with bayonets. Major Lemuel P. Montgomery was the first American soldier killed when he reached the top of the barricade.

During the day, Jackson's troops killed at least 800 Red Sticks at Horseshoe Bend. American casualties totaled 50 dead and 150 wounded. Some of the Indian dead included children and women caught in the crossfire. Jackson later admitted, "I lament that two or three women and children were killed by accident." Some warriors, including Menewa, managed to escape, by swimming across the Tallapoosa River. Some accounts say they hid beneath the water and breathed through reeds until they thought it was safe to move. These Indians continued to harass settlers, but lacked strength to confront American troops. The Battle of Horseshoe Bend was the final confrontation in the Creek War of 1813–1814, effectively breaking the formerly powerful Creek Nation apart. Jackson was promoted to the rank of brigadier general as a reward for this military success.

Jackson sent Major General Thomas Pinckney this battle report:

> On the Battle ground, in the Bend of the Talapoose, 28th March, 1814.
>
> Maj. Gen. Pinckney,
>
> Sir—I feel particularly happy in being able to communicate to you the fortunate eventation [sic] of my expedition to the Tallapoosie. I reached the head near Emue fau (called by the whites the Horse-shoe) about 10 o'clock on the forenoon of yesterday, where I found the strength of the neighboring towns collected: expecting our approach, they had gathered from Oakfuskee, Oakahoga, New Yaagau, Hillibees, the Fish Pond and Eufalee towns, to the number it is said of 1000. It is difficult to conceive a situation more eligible for defence than the one they had chosen, or one rendered more secure by the skill with which they had erected their breastwork. It was from 5 to 8 feet high, and extended across the point in much a direction, as that a force approaching it would be exposed to a double fire while they lay in perfect security behind. A cannon planted at one extremity could have raked it to no advantage.
>
> Determining to exterminate them, I detached Gen. Coffee with the mounted and nearly the whole of the Indian force early on the morning of yesterday to cross the river about two miles below their encampment, and to surround the bend in such a manner, as that none of them should escape by attempting to cross the river. With the infantry I proceeded slowly and in order along the point of land which led to the front of their brestwork; having planted my cannon, [one six and one three pounder] on an eminence at the distance of 150 to 200

yards from it. I opened a very brisk fire, playing upon the enemy with the muskets and rifles whenever they showed themselves beyond it; this was kept up with short interruptions for about two hours, when a part of the Indian force and captain Russell's and Lt. Bean's companies of spies, who had accompanied Gen. Coffee, crossed over in canoes to the extremity of the bend, and set fire to a few of the buildings which were there situated; they then advanced with great gallantry towards the breastwork, and commenced a spirited fire upon the enemy behind it. Finding that this force, not-withstanding the bravery they displayed, was wholly insufficient to dislodge them, and that Gen. Coffee had entirely secured the opposite bank of the river, I now determined to take their works by storm. The men by whom this was to be effected had been waiting with impatience to recieve [sic] the order, and hailed it with acclamation.

The spirit which animated them was a pure augury of the success which was to follow. The history of warfare I think furnishes few instances of a more brilliant attack—the regulars led on by their intrepid and skillful commander Col. Williams, and by the gallant Major Montgomery, soon gained possession of the works in the midst of a most tremendous fire from behind them, and the militia of the venerable General Doherty's brigade accompanied them in the charge with a vivacity and firmness which would have done honor to regulars. The enemy were completely routed. Five hundred and fifty seven were left dead on the peninsula, and a great number were killed by the horsemen in attempting to cross the river—it is believed that not more than twenty have escaped.

The fighting continued with some severity about five hours, but we continued to destroy many of them who had concealed themselves under the banks of the river until we were prevented by the night. This morning we killed 16 who had been concealed. We took about 250 prisoners, all women and children except two or three. Our loss is 106 wounded and 25 killed. Major M'Intosh [the Cowetau] who joined my army with a part of his tribe, greatly distinguished himself. When I get an hour's leisure I will send you a more detailed account.

According to my original purpose, I commenced my return march to Fort Williams to-day, and shall, if I find sufficient supplies there, hasten to the Hickory ground. The power of the Creeks is I think forever broken.

I have the honor to be, with great respect, your obedient servant,

Andrew Jackson

On April 2, 1814, Major General Thomas Pinckney wrote Georgia governor Peter Early in Milledgeville that "I have the honor of enclosing to your excellency the official account of a decisive victory over the hostile Creek Indians." He continued, reporting that this battle success was

achieved by the military talents and enterprize [sic] of Gen. Jackson, supported by the distinguished valor and good conduct of the gallant troops under his command. While the sigh of humanity will escape for this profuse effusion of human blood, which results from the savage principle of our enemy, neither to give nor accept quarter—and while every American will deeply lament the loss of our meritorious fellow soldiers who have fallen in this contest, we have ample cause of gratitude to the Giver of all victory for thus continuing his protection to our women and children, who would otherwise be exposed to the indiscriminate havoc of the tomahawk and all the horrors of savage warfare.

Jackson's and Pickney's letters and news about Horseshoe Bend were published in the April 18, 1814, *National Daily Intelligencer* in Washington, D.C.

The Battle of Horseshoe Bend has been mythologized and many legends circulated, such as the tales of Jackson speaking to his troops from the "Jackson Oak," Davy Crockett fighting at Horseshoe Bend, and Cherokee Chief Junaluska saving Jackson's life during the battle. In fact, the tree identified as Jackson Oak was too young to have even sprouted when the battle happened. Jackson would have been physically incapable to have climbed a tree then. Crockett had been mustered out of service in December

WILLIAM MCINTOSH. He led the friendly Creek Native Americans who fought at the Battle of Horseshoe Bend and was rewarded for his allegiance with the Americans.

1813. And Junaluska's role has been depicted solely in Cherokee tales and is not cited in primary records.

By August 1814, Weatherford, who had not been at Horseshoe Bend, but learned his capture was required for peace for his people, went to Jackson's headquarters at Fort Jackson (the Fort Toulouse site) to surrender. He expected to be executed and only asked for clemency for the Creek children and women. Impressed by Weatherford's courage, Jackson pardoned his enemy if he agreed to stop waging war and permitted him to stay at Jackson's Tennessee home, the Hermitage, where they discussed American-Indian diplomatic concerns. Weatherford later returned to southern Alabama where he was a planter.

The Treaty of Fort Jackson, signed on August 9, 1814, resulted in both Upper and Lower Creeks ceding approximately 23 million acres in Alabama and Georgia to the United States. Soon, white settlers began migrating to the captured territory. Although the Creek Nation lost its power, many Indians remained at settlements along the Tallapoosa River. Some joined Indians in Florida to fight the Seminole Wars. McIntosh was commissioned as a brigadier general for cooperating with Americans and signing the Treaty of Fort Jackson.

The Battle of Horseshoe Bend preceded significant War of 1812 engagements, such as the Battle of New Orleans, which enabled the United States to defeat the British. General Andrew Jackson's victory at Horseshoe Bend resulted in him being featured in national and regional newspapers, and his heroism at Horseshoe Bend transformed his life. Many Americans admired the valiant Jackson and voted for him when he later campaigned for the United States presidency. In 1828, Jackson was elected the nation's seventh president.

Several Alabama counties were named for Horseshoe Bend heroes, and some Horseshoe Bend veterans settled near the battlefield. Several continued serving in the military. A few, such as Samuel Houston, won political offices, including terms as governors and senators. Others, such as the Walker brothers, headed west, seeking adventure, opportunity, and wealth. They blended into their communities and became pack train guides, farmers, entrepreneurs, mountain men, husbands, and fathers. Horseshoe Bend was a memory for them, not an identity. Scars and aches reminded them of that March morning. Dr. Ashbel Smith said Houston's arrow wound "remained a running sore to his grave."

On February 12, 1825, McIntosh convinced 12 chiefs to sign the Treaty of Indian Springs, ceding all Creek territory east of the Mississippi River, including the Tallapoosa River settlements, to the United States. Thirty-six chiefs and Secretary of War John C. Calhoun did not support this treaty, but it became legal after United States Senate ratification. Angered that McIntosh accepted $25,000 for arranging passage of this treaty, the Creek National Council asked Menewa to murder McIntosh. McIntosh was killed by gunfire on May 1, 1825, when he was fleeing from his house that Menewa had set ablaze.

In 1830, President Jackson signed the Indian Removal Bill, which legalized relocating tribes east of the Mississippi River. The United States government began surveying Creek lands in 1831 for possible white settlements. The Cusseta Treaty of 1832 ceded Creek lands east of the Tallapoosa River to the United States. Each Creek head of household was allowed 320 acres, and chiefs received 640 acres. Settlers bid on lots located on this land during a public auction. The Kowaliga Creeks chose lands throughout the area that the lake would ultimately cover. Conflicts with whites resulted in the government expelling the Indians.

By 1836, most of the Tallapoosa River Indians were forcibly removed to western reservations on the Trail of Tears, named that because so many Indian deaths resulted from the rigors of traveling. Many of the Alabama Indians were relocated to Mobile where they were placed on ships. Those vessels transported the Indians to New Orleans. From there, they went up the Mississippi River on steamboats to Arkansas where they were moved overland to Oklahoma Territory. Other groups of Indians were moved north by ground transportation through Tennessee to Arkansas. Tallapoosa River Creeks took their customs and practices from Kowaliga Creek and other areas later flooded by lake water to their new homes in the Indian Territory. After these people left, floods revealed Native American relics to remind later generations of the lake area's first residents. Land records in Elmore County's probate office often include the names of original Creek property owners.

WEAPONS FROM THE BATTLE OF HORSESHOE BEND SITE. People found these artifacts, which are preserved at the Horseshoe Bend National Military Park.

3. PIONEERS BEFORE LAKE MARTIN

Settlers swarmed into the Tallapoosa River area after the Creeks were removed. As the American population grew, migrants moved westward, seeking space and opportunities on the frontier. Millions of stories could be told about the people who lived in the Lake Martin area before the dam and lake were created. The following vignettes reveal how people lived, formed communities, and influenced the land (later submerged beneath the lake) during the nineteenth and early twentieth centuries.

Alabama fever struck many Georgians and Carolinians who traveled by wagon, stagecoach, and on foot on paths and westward routes, including the Old Georgia Road (which passed through the Kowaliga area) and the Federal Road. Pioneers cleared the woods and Creek villages to build houses and plant fields. Settlers named communities for favorite places back east, family members, geographical landmarks, or for humorous reasons (resulting in such towns as Flea Hop in Elmore County). Many Native American place names were also retained.

Early settlers represented a variety of trades. Farmers cultivated fields. Doctors medicated and healed the sick. Ministers rode circuits to save souls and comfort the lonely. Craftsmen produced items to meet people's daily needs. Country store clerks stocked essential goods. Tinsmiths peddled their wares. Lawyers defended or prosecuted accused thieves, criminals, and murderers. Laborers processed timber at sawmills and turpentine works. Most pioneers led hardscrabble lives. They had limited financial resources, but plenty of dreams and determination.

Tallapoosa County was formed from Creek territory in December 1832. Thirty-four years later, Elmore County was created from Tallapoosa, Coosa, Montgomery, and Autauga Counties. Dadeville and Youngsville were the main pioneer settlements with many smaller communities developing near creeks and roads. Ferries carried people, livestock, and goods across the Tallapoosa River. A visiting New Yorker named Dubois described his cousin's "saw" and "gris" mills at Tallapoosa Falls and "Solgahatchee" in an October 8, 1841 diary entry. Carpenters built the Oakachoy Covered Bridge, which still stands. Schools were available throughout the area, including the Southern Industrial Institute (Lyman Ward Academy) and Kowaliga Academic and Industrial Institute, founded for African-American children.

John H. Broadnax surveyed Dadeville in 1836. An Indian trading post, Dadeville was the center of local commerce, and lumber, cotton, livestock, tin, and asbestos were traded at the town's markets. Dadeville, Alabama, was named in honor of Major Francis Langhorne Dade, whose death in 1835, while commanding American military forces that Indians massacred in Florida, marked the beginning of the Second Seminole War. That battle was the first in a seven-year war that secured America's territorial rights to settle Florida safely. Dade had never visited Tallapoosa County.

Dadeville was a stagecoach stop between Montgomery and Georgia, and traders and travelers also passed through Dadeville on the Tennessee Road. The courthouse square area often was thick with livestock and goods being transported through frontier Alabama. Racetracks and cock-fighting pens provided entertainment on the town's periphery.

Youngsville was named for pioneer settler James Young. In 1873, Youngsville citizens agreed to call their town Alexander City in recognition of Edward Porter Alexander, the

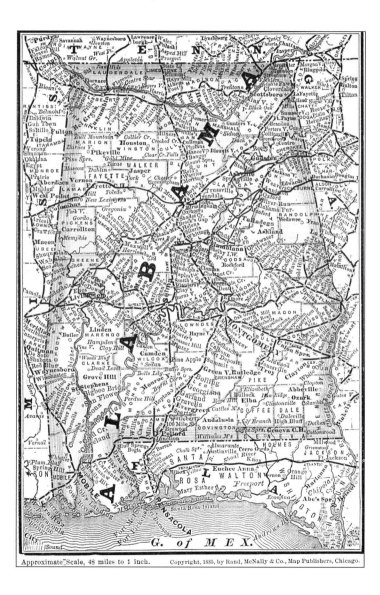

1885 ALABAMA RAILROAD MAP. Rail roads provided transportation to the communities that once existed where the lake is now.

president of the Savannah and Memphis Railroad, which built a line from Opelika to Alexander City. Railroad access transformed Alexander City into a major market in the region. By the twentieth century, Russell Mills and Avondale Mills appropriated local cotton and water resources to offer employment opportunities.

Dudleyville's Abraham M. Mordecai, a Pennsylvania native and Alabama's first Jewish resident, was one of the lake area's most interesting settlers. His life reveals details about the Creeks in addition to insights on how early Alabama settlers existed. In 1783, Mordecai, seeking new adventures, relocated to Buzzard Roost in Georgia to work as an Indian trader. He married a Creek woman and practiced Creek customs. The Creeks formally adopted him. Mordecai participated in an initiation ceremony in which he imbibed the ritual "black drink" and was christened with the Creek name Miccogee,

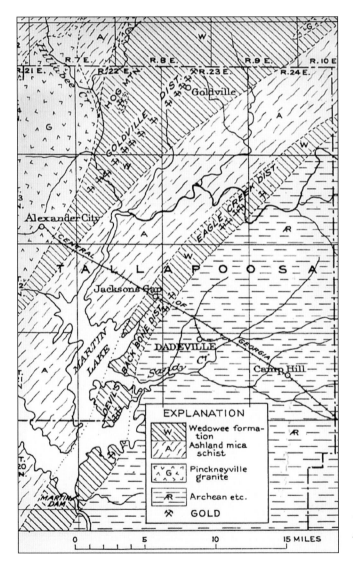

TALLAPOOSA COUNTY GOLD MAP. A geological survey documented where gold deposits were located in the Lake Martin area.

meaning "Little Chief." Because of his familiarity with Indian customs and ability to converse in their native tongues, American officials asked Mordecai to negotiate ransoms for white captives, especially kidnapped women and children, held by Indians and arrange for their safe release. He frequently communicated with southern Indians for Indian Agent James Seagrove, traveling on peace missions with Timothy Barnard. The names of Mordecai and Barnard are often recorded in the published American State Papers regarding Indian Affairs.

About 1789, Mordecai moved to Line Creek near present-day Montgomery, Alabama. Sources state that he was the first native-born American citizen to live in Alabama— most early settlers were foreign-born immigrants—as well as the state's first cotton cultivator. In 1804, Mordecai arranged for the first cotton gin in the Mississippi Territory to be built after he was encouraged by Agent for Indian Affairs, Colonel Benjamin J. Hawkins, who believed that the gin would teach Indians about efficient and profitable agricultural methods. Mordecai secured the approval of Creek chiefs. He erected the gin on the first eastern bluff below the junction of the Coosa and Tallapoosa Rivers known as Red Fields.

Lyons and Barnett, manufacturers from Georgia, built the gin and conveyed their tools, materials, and gin saw on pack horses to the site. The gin was located next to a racetrack owned by Charles Weatherford (Red Eagle's father) where he raced his selectively bred horses for monetary bets and personal pride. Horse thieves from Georgia tested the speed of stolen steeds as they fled the track area. Indian women transported their villages' cotton to Mordecai in canoes they navigated down the Tallapoosa River. He bought the fibrous bolls and ginned them, filling his yard with processed bales. The bagged cotton was then shipped by boats and horses to major cities to sell for a profit.

In 1812, Mordecai moved with his family to Tallapoosa County. According to his tombstone, he served with Private Thomas's Company of the Georgia Militia in the War of 1812. Mordecai roamed the countryside before the Creek War in 1813 during which he served as trail guide for the Georgia Militia under General John Floyd. He guided 950 white soldiers and 450 Creeks, including such prominent warriors as William McIntosh, by the Tallapoosa River toward the hostile Red Stick Creek village of Autossee.

Floyd's troops were able to move at night because of Mordecai's tracking skills and arrived at the town by dawn on November 29, 1813, surprising the Red Sticks. The Battle of Autossee was a success for Floyd whose forces were able to destroy the hostile Indians' town. Mordecai also served under Floyd at his last battle at Calabee Creek in January 1814 where the Red Sticks were routed in the swamp. Mordecai reportedly fought in the Battle of Horseshoe Bend two months later, although he may actually have continued his services as a guide or scout.

After the war, in 1814, Andrew Jackson assigned Indian boundaries, and Mordecai settled his family in the Creek Nation. When the Creeks were forcibly removed in 1836, however, Mordecai decided not to go with them. His wife had already died, and his children had grown up and left the area. As an American citizen, the aging Mordecai did not try to secure any land under the 1832 treaty, which legally opened the area to white settlement. Instead, he relocated to Dudleyville, a thriving community, to open a trading store.

The town was named for Peter Dudley who had established the community's first trading post. Dudleyville flourished in the aftermath of the Creek Indian Wars and the 1832 treaty. Numerous stores, churches, schools, and homes lined its streets, and the town's population swelled. Mordecai operated his store while he was physically able, but his advanced age slowed him down and reduced the amount of money he could eke out from his crafty trading. He lived in a log house, which resembled an Indian hut, that his neighbor James Moore, an original settler of Montgomery Bluff, arranged to be built. Citizens of Dudleyville charitably gave Mordecai food, and he reportedly said grace before every meal to praise their generosity.

Predicting his death was near and not wanting to cause his neighbors and friends inconvenience, Mordecai arranged for a walnut coffin to be made by a Mr. Clayton, probably a local carpenter, several years before he died. Mordecai kept the coffin in his house by his bed. He also had a Bible and some furniture and bottles, including an earthenware rum jug. Although he prepared to die, Mordecai exhibited a lively attitude, walking into town every day, his long white hair billowing in the breeze, to hear the latest news. He enjoyed sitting in the sunshine or by the tavern fire, sharing town gossip with his neighbors, although he was somewhat deaf from an infectious cold he had suffered.

Ambitious newspaper reporters sought out Mordecai to learn about his 50 years of experiences with the Creek Indians. The *Columbus (Georgia) Enquirer* printed an article based on an interview with Mordecai on February 22, 1843, and historian Albert J. Pickett wrote a detailed description of Mordecai in the October 4, 1847 *Flag and Advertiser*. He colorfully characterized Mordecai:

> The old man was of low statue, round and compactly built, his limbs and body being admirably knit together. While his head bore the emblems of age as to colour, it was nevertheless covered with a profusion of hair. His forehead was well formed, his mouth large and expressive, his eyes of a deep hazel hue, which ever and anon would sparkle like diamonds, at the mention of old occurrences.

Pickett shared several conversations he had with Dudleyville's spry Indian trader, and Mordecai was a primary source for Pickett's history of Alabama, which focused on the Creek Nation and interaction of whites and Indians on the frontier. Mordecai told Pickett that he believed that Alabama's Indians were descended from Jews because they used the word "yavoyaha," which meant "Jehovah" or "Great Spirit," in the Green Corn Dance, which celebrated bountiful harvests. The theory that American Indians were of Jewish descent was a popular topic of debate among nineteenth-century historians and anthropologists, and Mordecai's insight, as a Jew, was of interest.

Mordecai died in 1850 and was buried between two hickory trees in the Dudleyville Cemetery, about 7 miles east of Horseshoe Bend. His grave was unmarked until 1932 when the Tohopeka Chapter of the Daughters of the American Revolution and Peter Brannon of the Alabama State Department of Archives and History arranged for a marble marker to be placed on the burial site. Nearby in the Dudleyville cemetery are the graves of Major Lemuel P. Montgomery, the first soldier killed at the Battle of Horseshoe Bend, and of Dudley, the town's namesake, which is about 30 feet from Mordecai's grave and covered with a pile of stones. On June 3, 1839, Montgomery and another soldier killed at the Horseshoe Bend barricade had been exhumed from their battlefield graves and reburied with military honors accompanied by speeches, a band tribute, and gun salute.

Soon after Mordecai's demise, Dudleyville's preeminence faded when the Central of Georgia Railroad reached Dadeville, and many Dudleyville stores and residents relocated to that town. A fire razed Dudleyville's commercial district during the Civil War, assuring that it would lose its status as a prospering village. Mordecai's trading post in Dudleyville no longer stands, but the legends about the rugged old Indian trader remain as a testament to the challenges and character of the Alabama frontier.

An early 1840s gold rush attracted hopeful prospectors to Tallapoosa County, and Goldville, incorporated in 1843, was the nucleus of this rush. Approximately 3,500 people came to extract gold veins and hunt for loose gold. Miners lived in tents, and saloons, stores, and hotels were quickly erected to serve the mining community. Goldville was one of early Alabama's most populated communities. Gold mines were set up after early settlers discovered gold in area creeks, including Kowaliga. Miners sifted through pans of sand from streams for gold. They used shovels and picks to dig trenches, pits, shafts, and underground mines.

Bankers and investors from New York and London were interested in Tallapoosa mining properties. State geologist Michael Tuomey assessed the Silver Hill Gold Mine on Copper Creek in 1845. He evaluated the vein to be 2 feet thick, becoming thinner but more valuable at depths of 12 feet. The gold vein extended as far as 80 feet deep.

TALLAPOOSA MINING COMPANY. After gold was discovered in east Alabama, including Tallapoosa County, various methods of finding and extracting gold from the earth were used by hardworking and innovative miners.

When gold was discovered in California, many Alabama gold miners traveled west, planning to benefit from their experiences in the Tallapoosa gold fields. Thomas Taylor Farrow owned the Farrow Gold Mining Company (near Curry's Camp after the lake filled) in the late nineteenth and early twentieth centuries. He invented a self-powered railway for his mine in which each car could transport one ton of ore. Farrow also used a water-powered stamp machine.

Some Tallapoosa gold mines continued operating into the late 1930s. However, operating costs usually exceeded profits and this caused most to close. The lake partially or completely submerged many of the gold sites. The Devil's Backbone gold district extends from Martin Dam along the lakeshore to Jackson's Gap.

Although he did not seek gold, Johnson Jones Hooper traveled in Tallapoosa County as a census taker and lawyer during the 1830s to 1850s. He frequently boarded at the United States Hotel built at Dadeville in 1836. The inn, owned and run by the Dennis family, was often referred to by their name. At that two-story wooden structure, Johnson penned humorous tales about his adventures in the county. The stories were set at Tallapoosa County sites, including the hotel, and featured its unique and colorful residents.

Pickett considered Hooper Alabama's most outstanding journalist, and one newspaper emphatically stated that "the world does not contain a better nor a braver heart than throbs in the bosom of J.J. Hooper." Witticisms and humorous tales that enthralled the nation flowed from Hooper's pen. The *Alabama Journal*, in a passage, possibly

JOHNSON J. HOOPER HISTORICAL MARKER. Dadeville is proud of its literary heritage, especially Hooper's stories, which documented pioneer history.

written by Hooper poking fun at himself, described him as "A kiln-dried specimen of humanity, about 5 feet 10 inches in height; a cross between an Egyptian mummy and a shriveled pumpkin."

From the age of 11, Hooper worked as a "printer's devil" for his father's newspaper in North Carolina, setting type and occasionally composing contributions. In September 1835, he moved to live with his brother George in the frontier town of Lafayette, Alabama. He read law with his brother, helping him with his law practice that extended to Dadeville, Dudleyville, and the settlements that once stood where Lake Martin is now. Hooper traveled throughout Alabama's remote frontier area, conversing with clients and gathering information. His wit, humor, and patient, listening ear won him countless friends from all social classes and professions.

During his travels, Hooper became familiar with the Creek Indians and fascinated with the local Indians, especially their ball games, dances, campfires, and council meetings such as one held in Tallapoosa County's Dudley's Store. He also encountered a variety of tough, rugged, and somewhat charming characters—gamblers, highwaymen, and bandits—that made the frontier so colorful. Their lewd, crude, and rough lifestyles often included cheating, swearing, and fighting. The backwoods social life was devoted to corn whiskey, card games, and boasts that Hooper described in his stories.

Hooper also met his brother George's friends, including original Dadeville settlers Bird H. Young, Charles Stine, Edward Hanrick, Isaiah Perry, and John J. Holly. Those men liked Hooper, and he gained a reputation as being a jolly and fun-loving person, acquiring the nickname Jonce. In autumn 1938, Hooper was appointed as notary public in Tallapoosa County, serving until 1840 when he was deputized as assistant marshal and census taker for the county. His job required him to count all human and chicken inhabitants of the county, earning him the name "the chicken man."

Many county residents regarded Hooper with suspicion, believing that his true purpose was to estimate taxes owed. Hooper was often greeted with surly dogs that evasive masters ordered to attack him. Hooper considered his job tedious and too much work for too little pay. He counted 2,318 white men, 2,106 white women, 2,013 slaves, and 9 free blacks. Records do not indicate how many chickens he managed to document.

Hooper entered into a legal practice with his friend Charles Stine in Dadeville in 1841. It was the first law practice in that city, but only attracted a few clients; by 1842, Hooper returned to work with his brother as a legal partner.

Some nineteenth-century biographies of Hooper suggest that during this period he edited the *Dadeville Banner*, but historian W. Stanley Hoole disputes this claim, noting that the newspaper did not begin publication until 1852. Perhaps Hooper briefly edited a newspaper of a similar title, of which copies have not survived for modern historians to examine. Documents show that Hooper did purchase clothing, horse saddlery, knives, and watermelon while he lived in Dadeville.

Hooper did edit the *East Alabamian* at Lafayette. In August 1843, he published his first humorous piece, "Taking the Census in Alabama," signing it "By a Chicken Man of 1840." He wrote the story because he needed to fill space in the paper and to entertain readers. Using local dialects, colloquialisms, idioms, and vernacular speech that he had often listened to in a tavern or at a campfire, he described a sincere census taker's (unidentified but understood to be Hooper) efforts to count every nose and beak in the county. Hooper embellished the census taker's frustrations when his subjects refused to cooperate.

He chronicled how sharp-tongued, elderly widows were reluctant to reveal their age. Hooper told how the census taker frequently departed homes at a gallop as snarling hounds chased after him and epithets were hurled by those he had just tallied. He humorously narrated how when the census taker stated that he needed to count their chickens to estimate their value, many people scattered corn at his feet and he was soon inundated with squawking, feather-shedding, pecking poultry.

Hooper also revealed how he was tricked by a man who told him a safe place to ford a creek, when instead, a deep hole was located at the crossing. The census taker's horse panicked as its hooves suddenly lost contact with the creek bed. After the census taker and horse extricated themselves from the murky waters, the census taker overheard a conversation that stated the "helpful" man had bragged that he would play a practical joke on the chicken man. For revenge, the census taker found the man and hinted that while trying to escape the swirling waters, he had lost a pouch filled with gold. He promised to give the man half of the contents if he found the bag and brought it to Dadeville. The satisfaction that his tormentor would soon be literally "all wet" smoothed the chicken man's ruffled feathers.

William T. Porter, editor of *The Spirit of the Times*, read "Taking the Census in Alabama" in a New York City newspaper and reprinted it in his magazine in September 1843, stating, "This Hooper is a clever man." His periodical was primarily a sporting journal that featured the Southwest, which at that time consisted of Alabama, Mississippi, Arkansas, and settlements on their frontiers. Many of the magazine's articles were in fact tall tales, exaggerating hunting and fishing catches. Porter was intensely interested in securing Hooper as a regular correspondent from Alabama to supply additional humorous stories.

In his travels, Hooper had often heard local boasts and yarns and collected these narratives to retell verbally and in print. He also drew upon his personal experiences, such as a story about a hunting trip in which he wildly exaggerated his encounter with a bear and the amount of game killed. Hooper included a tale about how his clever dog Pont stepped on sleeping ducks' tail feathers and then crushed their heads in his jaw to silence any warning quacks to nearby birds.

Hooper's most famous fictional character was Captain Simon Suggs who starred in a series of stories in the *East Alabamian*, beginning in December 1844 and reprinted in Southern newspapers and Porter's periodical. Suggs's life philosophy was "It's good to be shifty in a new country" and "It is right and proper that one should live as merrily and as comfortably as possible at the expense of others." Suggs was considered a roguish rascal who outsmarted and outwitted Indians, law enforcement officials, and settlers with his shrewd cunning. In a time when lawlessness and individualism prevailed on the frontier, Suggs's exploits reflected common occurrences in the backwoods. In the stories, Suggs interacted with Tallapoosa County Indians and gullible settlers, fleecing them of property and valuables. Despite his questionable activity, Suggs was considered a heroic figure to his neighbors and kin.

PIONEER'S GRAVE MARKER. This marker is on a Lake Martin island.

For instance, he was elected a militia captain of the Tallapoosa Volunteers when his neighbors were afraid of an impending Indian raid. Suggs, lucking out as he so often did in his adventures, never had to fight any Indians because the raid did not occur. He enjoyed his enhanced status as a protector and military leader, boasting about his as-yet unproven courage and appropriated his unearned military title.

Many readers who knew Hooper believed that Suggs was a composite of the author. Descriptions of Suggs matched those of his creator, and his antics resembled some of Hooper's experiences and behavior. Some readers also recognized that many of Suggs's traits were common to those of Bird H. Young. An Alexander City settler, Young owned a 600-acre farm and was an unsavory but well-liked local character fondly regarded as a practical joker, defrauder, and gambler. Young also detected similarities between himself and Suggs and even considered suing Hooper for defamation. He was most angered and threatened to flog Hooper when a reference to Mrs. Suggs was viewed as a personal attack on his wife. Although Young was joking about many of his threats to sue Hooper, he demanded an apology for the Mrs. Suggs comments and Hooper printed a retraction letter in which he stated that Mrs. Suggs was not Mrs. Young and how much he respected the latter woman.

In the summer of 1845, the Simon Suggs stories were printed in *The Spirit of the Times*, and Hooper received national recognition for his talent as a writer and journalist. Newspapers across the country reprinted Hooper's stories, praising his insight and skill with dialect and interpreting Alabama's frontier people. His story "How Simon Suggs Raised Jack" was included in the book *The Big Bear of Arkansas* edited by T.B. Thorpe. Hooper's humorous sketches were compiled into one volume entitled *The Adventures of Simon Suggs*, which was published in 11 editions from 1845 to 1856. The first issue consisted of 3,000 copies, and 5,000 more were printed by fall 1845 because of the national attention and regard for the quality of Hooper's narratives.

Although Porter, as well as other editors, demanded more stories, Hooper concentrated on legal work to earn income. He was elected solicitor of the Ninth Judicial Circuit, referred to as the "Bloody Ninth" because of the lawless behavior of some of its rowdy and uncivilized inhabitants. The circuit encompassed Tallapoosa County, as well as Macon, Russell, Chambers, Randolph, and Talladega Counties. Hooper based his headquarters in Dadeville's Dennis Hotel when he rode the circuit to prosecute offenders who had committed crimes against the state. He represented the state in county courthouses, including the one built in Dadeville in 1839.

During his travels of the circuit, Hooper met a variety of swindlers, orators, peddlers, lawyers, and other professionals on the frontier and in the hotels and taverns that were enlivened with raucous noise and laughter late into the night. From his observations and participation in poker games, as well as encountering monkey grinders and trained bear acts, Hooper had a wealth of information for stories, including "A Ride with Old Kit Kuncker" and "The Widow Rugby's Husband." Suggs outsmarted the Tallapoosa County sheriff in "The Muscadine Story." One Hooper tale was based on details of the Battle of Horseshoe Bend. In 1859, Hooper edited and wrote the introduction to *Woodward's Reminiscences of the Creek, or Muskogee Indians*.

Hooper is often referred to as Alabama's Mark Twain. Incidentally, Twain read and was influenced by Hooper's stories as can be seen in passages of Huckleberry Finn that are strikingly similar to Suggs's exploits. Hooper's amusing accounts of Alabama's local people have preserved their speech, culture, and lives for future generations to learn about their state's picturesque past.

In a more serious vein, Philip Madison Shepard opened the Graefenberg Medical Institute, Alabama's first medical school, at Dadeville in 1852. Antebellum Alabamians, especially in rural regions, desperately needed doctors to provide basic health care. Shepard received his medical education at the Georgia Medical College at Augusta, moved to Alabama in 1836, and moved his medical practice to Dadeville one decade later. By summer 1851, Shepard placed an advertisement in the *Montgomery Advertiser and State Gazette*, announcing the opening of the Graefenberg Infirmary and Hydropathic Establishment, where "Allopathy, Hydropathy, Homeopathy, and Botany would be taught scientifically." The school's name was borrowed from an Austrian medical institute that specialized in hydrotherapy, a popular treatment of that era that consisted of bathing in warm, soothing waters.

Shepard served as proprietor and professor of the Graefenberg Medical Institute, which was a family-run business. Shepard named his half-brother W. Banks president of the board of trustees, and his other half-brother J.T. Banks and Mrs. Shepard's cousin M.L. Fielder as trustees. Dr. James I. Shackelford and William M.A. Mitchell also joined the board. At the same time, Shepard started and served as proprietor of the Winston

Male College (a military school) and the Octavia Walton Lee Vert Normal College for Young Ladies on Graefenberg's campus. At first Shepard was the school's only professor. When his son John graduated from Graefenberg in 1855 at the age of 18, he joined the faculty, as did Philip Madison Jr. (class of 1858), and Orlando Tyler (class of 1860), who at age 17 became Graefenberg's professor of Obstetrics and Diseases of Women and Children. Shepard's daughter Louise also received her degree from Graefenberg, supposedly making her the first woman graduate of a Southern medical school, but she was discouraged by negative public sentiment and abandoned her medical career.

Graefenberg had two sessions—May to October and November to March—and students could graduate after one session if they could pass the final examination, which consisted of 5,000 questions proctored by the trustees in a process that lasted three days and nights and was presented publicly. Each student paid $135 per session for lodging, washing, and a diploma, $60 for tuition ($30-40 during the summer), and a $10 library fee if he or she had to repeat a course. Students attended lectures, answered tests, and participated in laboratory clinics. Shepard often took his pupils to visit patients admitted to Graefenberg's six treatment cottages or in their own homes.

Graefenberg was housed in a three-story building and had a library with standard items such as encyclopedias, textbooks, and medical journals, as well as an anatomical museum, auditorium, classrooms, and an herbarium. Students were supplied with scientific equipment and medical devices and were able to practice dissection, becoming familiar with human anatomy, on skeletons and cadavers obtained from robbed graves, executed criminals from area prisons, or deceased vagrants delivered from Montgomery and New Orleans and stored in metal-lined vats.

During each session, approximately 10 to 20 students lived in the dormitory adjacent to the Shepard's home and ate meals with the family. They also helped tend the herb garden to provide pharmaceuticals. Shepard insisted that his pupils regularly read the Bible, emphasizing that they lead simple, healthy, and spiritual lives.

In 1861, Shepard accidentally sliced his finger while performing an autopsy and subsequently died from blood poisoning. He was buried in the Shepard family cemetery located 1 mile north of Dadeville. Surviving family members were unable to schedule classes at Graefenberg during the Civil War, but they hoped to reopen the school after hostilities ceased. Unfortunately, in 1873, the school was razed in a fire.

East Alabamians regarded military service seriously. The antebellum militia companies, the Emuckfau Guards and the Horseshoe Rangers, protected Tallapoosa residents, and some area residents fought in the Seminole and Mexican Wars. Approximately 2,800 Tallapoosa County men served with Confederate forces fighting in the Civil War. Some men enlisted in other counties or in Tennessee when Alabama could not supply all of the Tallapoosa volunteers. The Tallapoosa Thrashers fought for Company K of the 38th Tennessee Volunteers.

Soldiers posed for daguerreotypes to give to family and sweethearts before joining comrades at local military camps. Then, the men boarded trains or marched on foot to serve at major battles and minor skirmishes. Some of the Tallapoosa men provided support services, guarding prisoners or preparing meals. Approximately 25 percent of

TALLAPOOSA TIMES
*ADVERTISEMENT. This ad was
printed to try and sell weapons prior
to the Civil War.*

Tallapoosa-area Civil War soldiers succumbed to battle wounds or disease while serving, but most men returned home to their families. Young men often headed west, seeking adventure and opportunities. The Lake Martin area has many Confederate veterans buried in country or city cemeteries.

Women, children, and men who were either too old or not healthy enough to fight tended the fields and defended the homefront. Communities honored their soldiers with ceremonies and presentation of hand-sewn flags. Some people manufactured rifles at the Tallassee Armory.

On April 28, 1864, Colonel Josiah Gorgas, chief of the Confederate Ordnance Bureau, had ordered Superintendent of Armories, Lieutenant Colonel James H. Burton, and his associate Captain C.P. Bolles to travel to Tallassee and survey the city to determine if it was a feasible site to relocate the Richmond Carbine Factory. Gorgas knew that Tallassee had an active cotton mill because it supplied Confederate uniforms and recognized that it was isolated in the Alabama interior, secure from enemy attack.

Burton and Bolles arrived in Tallassee on May 28 and quickly located the two mills of the Tallassee Falls Manufacturing Company. Local slaves had erected the building in 1844, constructing it with stones gathered along the Tallapoosa River. The company produced yarn, cotton, wool, thread, and cloth. After examining the mills for several days, Burton wrote Gorgas on June 1 in support of Tallassee as a desirable site to produce guns. The specific weapon to be constructed at Tallassee was a new model of the .58-caliber muzzle-loading carbine, which was promoted by General Robert E. Lee and Major General J.E.B. Stuart and had been chosen by the Confederate Board of Cavalry as a regular weapon. The gun measured slightly more than 40 inches long.

Burton secured the right of way to transportation, the rights to use river water and the water wheel, to build buildings, and to lease the building for the duration of the war, with exclusive use. Housing for transferred Richmond employees posed a significant problem. Burton stated that the town of Tallassee had entire cottages for factory workers, but none for armory workers. Burton wrote Gorgas that single men could arrange board and that he had leased "a sufficient number of town lots for the erection of twenty-five double tenements for families, giving to each family a garden spot of a full quarter of an acre. These lots are located in the best part of the town and are convenient to the factory."

Burton also conveyed a message that the sawmill at the factory produced an insufficient output for building materials and that they would have to ship in lumber. However, they would be able to make bricks on the site. They could ship lime on the railroad and other supplies could be brought on the river ferry. On May 8, Gorgas inscribed in his diary, "We are preparing to move our carbine factory with all the operations and their families, to Tallassee, Ala."

In July 1864, the future lake area witnessed Rousseau's Raiders sweep through Alabama to destroy Confederate industry and foodstuffs. Advancing toward Atlanta, Union Major General William T. Sherman devised a strategy to destroy Alabama railroads and military supplies to keep them from reinforcing Confederate General Joseph E. Johnston's army near Atlanta, Georgia. Union Major General Lovell H. Rousseau led 2,500 cavalrymen on a raid that began in Decatur, Alabama, on July 10. Six days later, five cavalry regiments of raiders reached Youngsville by evening. Captain Thomas A. Elkin, serving with the 5th Kentucky Cavalry, led raiders into Youngsville to seize bacon, cornmeal, and grain before destroying four warehouses. The men crossed the Tallapoosa River near Stowe's Ferry in the dark. "Ever after we referred to the crossing of that river in the night with shudders," Colonel William D. Hamilton, a 9th Ohio officer, remembered, saying the experience had been as "unpleasant as that of any battle." The raiders traveled to Dadeville then changed course to go east to Loachapoka.

As the raiders entered Loachapoka, they at last saw their objective—the Montgomery and West Point Railroad. Unknown to them, the Federals had come close to garnering a fine prize that would have given them headlines in every newspaper North and South: General Braxton Bragg, en route to Montgomery, had been through Loachapoka just five hours earlier. After destroying Loachapoka's rails and depot, the raiders skirmished with several companies of University of Alabama cadets and reserves near Chehaw Station. The raiders destroyed targeted sites in Auburn and Opelika before reaching Marietta, Georgia, on July 22. The raiders had passed within 10 miles of Tallassee, but did not harm the arsenal. The armory continued to produce carbines despite deficient materials. The black walnut wood to construct stocks was scarce, and scouts charged an exorbitant fee of $15 per day to look for it. Fearful after Rousseau's raid, Burton suggested:

> Since Tallassee has assumed a national importance by the location of an Armory there, I think some steps should be taken to render the employees efficient as troops. I therefore respectfully recommend that the officer in command at the Armory be instructed to organize a military company to be composed of Armory employees and to drill them, say, twice each week on Tuesdays & Fridays from 4 P.M. until 6 P.M. and that they be properly armed and equipped as infantry.

By October, approximately 100 carbines had been manufactured at Tallassee, but there was not enough steel to complete them for shipment.

In March and April 1865, armory workers dismantled equipment and prepared to evacuate when they learned that another Federal raid, known as Wilson's Raid, was scaring Alabamians. By April 9, the Tallassee Armory equipment began leaving Tallassee. Two groups of Wilson's raiders were near Tallassee, but passed north and south of the town. Records indicate that a total of 500 to 600 carbines were produced at the Tallassee Armory, and Tallassee Falls Manufacturing Company resumed operations after the war, making industrial fabrics.

The Tallapoosa River helped people recover, both economically and emotionally, from the Civil War. River picnics and parties foreshadowed future enjoyment of Lake Martin. T.C. Tucker of Opelika wrote this poem, called "Tallapoosa River," while relaxing at Cherokee Bluffs, and it was published in the *Tallapoosa Gazette* on June 4, 1880, at Dadeville:

> Tallapoosa, Tallapoosa—
> As I muse upon thy shore—
> Wilt thou tell me beauteous river,
> Of the ages gone before?
>
> When wast thou a little brook-let,
> Murmuring in thy song quite low;
> Sweetly winding in thy beauty
> Ages, ages long ago?
>
> When didst thou assume the grandeur,
> Now spread out before the eye?
> Was it 'fore the stars of heaven
> Decked the blue etherial sky?

Tell me of the mighty numbers,
Upon thy banks have played—
Of the Creeks and their forefathers—
They who on thy banks once strayed?

Tell me of that hardfought battle—
Sixty-seven years ago—
When brave Jackson and his heroes,
Made thy stream with blood to flow?

Down the banks at the old Horse-shoe,
Many an Indian brave;
Tallapoosa in thy bosom
Found a peaceful watery grave.

And, me thinks, I hear the cannon,
Still vibrating on the blast;
When the Creeks for home and country,
On the border fought his last.

Tallapoosa, Tallapoosa,
Be thy name in verse and song;
Ever chanted, beauteous river,
As time's circles roll along.

TALLAPOOSA RIVER, 1900. This picture was taken above the Tallassee Falls. The flowing river provided the area an abundance of water for work or play.

Farm owners and sharecroppers planted corn and cotton in nearby fields. Sugar cane patches produced juicy stalks that were crushed into syrup. Women churned butter from cows' milk, canned garden vegetables, gathered chicken eggs, and made jellies from fruits they grew or collected. Peach, scuppernong, and blackberry preserves were favorite jams. Picnics and square dances were favorite forms of entertainment. Sundays were serious days for worship. Gathering on church grounds in buggies, wagons, then Model Ts; "All-day singings with dinner on the grounds were popular, particularly the old fashioned Sacred Harp singings." At these, "With no instrumental accompaniment the singers would first sing the notes and follow with the words to each song."

The river expressed its contrary nature during the April 1886 flood, which changed the Tallapoosa River's channel course, creating new islands. The river level was raised 4 to 6

FLOODING OF THE TALLAPOOSA RIVER. This April 17, 1886 Harper's Weekly *cover depicted the swelling river.*

BATTLE OF HORSESHOE BEND MEMORIAL FESTIVITIES. People gathered to celebrate in 1912. Automobiles and wagons are parked in a field adjacent to the battle site where people attended the ceremony.

feet above previous flood levels. Observers from Montgomery's state capitol dome described the river "stretching away to the north and west, a lake of water fully ten miles square." People living along its banks were most at risk. Inmates of the Elmore County convict farm were rescued with rafts, and many prisoners escaped. Almost all of the bridges and mills on the Tallapoosa River were ruined, and thousands of livestock died. The United States Congress granted $300,000 to Alabama's flood victims. Natural disasters and storms often plagued the area, including a December 1919 flood in which torrential rainfall caused the river to rise 13 feet. Part of the Tallassee dam washed away, and its powerhouse was filled with flood debris, mud, trees, and cows. A March 28, 1920 tornado plucked area chickens clean.

Survival, courage, and patriotism were important traits to early lake-area residents. A.B. Meek had written an epic poem about Red Eagle in 1855, and his volume was reissued as a commemorative edition published by Montgomery's Paragon Press for the Horseshoe Bend centennial in 1914. Meek's book was distributed to Alabama schools and libraries and incorporated in classroom discussions. The centenary celebration was a major event for the future Lake Martin area. Andrew Jackson and his men were glorified as frontier military heroes. The Horseshoe Bend Memorial Commission organized anniversary memorials and printed programs. Observers arrived in Model Ts and horse-drawn wagons at the battle site to participate in the centennial's exercises. Thousands attended, and the *Birmingham News* reported that "Public houses and homes of Dadeville were crowded and overflowing with out-of-town people." Speakers narrated the site's significance and called for a "monument for the Indians as well as for our own heroes." A bronze tablet commemorating Horseshoe Bend was placed on the courthouse in Dadeville.

Tallapoosa area residents served in Company H of the 4th Alabama National Guard and the Alexander City Rifles infantry company. Marion Institute alumnus Captain Herman Winkler Thompson commanded the Tallapoosa National Guard forces sent to Nogales, Arizona, in 1916 to guard the Mexican border during the Mexican Revolution. One year later, the company was federalized as Company H, 167th United States Infantry, to serve in Europe after the United States entered World War I. That unit was incorporated into the 42nd Rainbow Division, and its men endured trench warfare during World War I. Tallapoosa soldiers also served in the 306th Engineer Regiment of the 81st Wildcat Division, building trenches, camouflaging sites, and stringing barbed wire and communication lines. Military officers praised Tallapoosa area doughboys for their combative prowess, awarding some of them honors such as the Distinguished Service Cross. Many local men were wounded or killed while fighting the Germans. The Alexander City American Legion Post is the namesake of Sergeant Henry Lorenzo Dabbs who died at St. Mihiel on September 13, 1918.

Beginning with the earliest settlements, people built fishing camps on the Tallapoosa River. Frank Wills Barnett wrote about Tallapoosa-area fishing in the December 31, 1922, *Montgomery Advertiser*, remarking that "Bass, perch, suckers and many kinds of catfish are found in the creeks. Opelousas cat fish are frequently caught weighing from twenty to thirty pounds." Occasionally, people caught big fish, including sea bass, that swam upriver from the coast to spawn prior to dam construction. One fisherman caught a 9-foot, 400-pound sturgeon south of Mitchell Dam.

Henry C. Jones, an Alabama Polytechnic Institute engineering alumnus, began pursuing hydroelectric power development in the 1890s. He studied electrical developments in both America and Europe. By 1896, Jones focused on the Tallapoosa River for dam projects because it was not navigable. At Cherokee Bluffs, the "river bed was solid rock, not too wide and was bordered by very steep, heavily timbered rocky bluffs on both sides, reaching some 200 feet above the river level on the east and some higher on the west bank." Jones arranged for feasibility studies and purchased land. His plans to build a 30-foot dam were interrupted by a yellow fever epidemic, which kept northeastern bankers from providing necessary funds. Jones contacted the Wall Street investment banking firm, Emerson McMillin & Company, which had been supportive of power utilities. As a result, the International Hydraulic Company was organized for Canadians to develop the site. When engineers hired by that group examined the Tallapoosa project, they were not supportive, saying the dam was "not feasible on account of low water records just then available, and which the Government started making of the Tallapoosa in 1896." Jones persevered, and in order to "offset the critical situation caused by these low water records, a higher dam was proposed and accepted at 50 feet."

Instead of the engineering team returning, Jones convinced the International Hydraulic Company president to evaluate the site personally. Jones later said that he paid the president's $200 daily fee plus costs while inspecting the site because "I recognized in him qualifications of vision and energy." He recalled that the president "saw for himself, was convinced and returned enthusiastic. Everything was lovely and contracts were being closed when something happened—the *Maine* blew up!" Jones received a letter from the International Hydraulic Company president, telling Jones to "Hold things together until we can whip the Spaniards and we will take matters up again." Instead, Cherokee Bluffs development was delayed, while other Alabama dams were considered on the Coosa River and at Tallassee.

The Alabama Power Company, founded by Captain William Patrick Lay, was also eager to develop the Tallapoosa River to generate hydroelectric power. In 1900, Jones and two Montgomery colleagues, James S. Pinckard and Jack Thorington, promoted Cherokee Bluffs. They lobbied the Alabama legislature to approve a special charter on December 8, 1900, for the Cherokee Development & Manufacturing Company to construct a dam on the Tallapoosa River at Double Bridge Ferry. The trio envisioned building a dam and generating plant at that site and convinced the United States government to survey the Tallapoosa and Coosa Rivers. As a result, a "splendid report of Major [Harley Bascom] Ferguson and his associates" was filed. The report

> laid out a plan for the development at Cherokee Bluffs, not only to store the flood waters for the generation of electric current, but to save great areas of the lower valleys from the effects of frequent and disastrous floods, and by releasing the stored waters in the dry seasons to greatly improve the navigation of the Alabama River.

On May 27, 1907, the Cherokee Development & Manufacturing Company was renamed the Birmingham, Montgomery & Gulf Power Company and accorded greater transmission generation possibilities. This group later was merged into the Alabama Power Company.

Developers recognized that the Tallapoosa River produced more power than the mills on the river utilized. Because the "laws of the State were deemed insufficient for the enlarged program foreseen by this and other groups then interested in power development," Thomas W. Martin explained, "the existing laws were revised in the Code of 1907." He credited Massey Wilson for the 1907 legislative improvements. Martin elaborated about the legal implications of and how the proposed Cherokee Bluffs project would affect the mills in Tallassee, including the one operated by the Mount Vernon-Woodberry Cotton Duck Company:

> It was obvious that the construction of a reservoir at Cherokee Bluffs would so regulate the flow of the river that the volume of power at this downstream dam would be vastly increased. In 1907 the Alabama Legislature accepted this fact and enlarged the power of eminent domain by conferring on power companies the right to acquire by condemnation "lands, hydraulic structures, water, or water rights of such cotton factory in excess of what is actually in use, or may be used at normal stages of the stream, for the operation of its plant as already established at the time the condemnation proceeding is commenced" (Code of Alabama 1907, Sec. 3627).

When hydroelectric power developers were unable to buy rights to excess power, they began condemnation proceedings.

Congress stated that construction for Lay Dam could proceed on March 4, 1907, although financial difficulties slowed that dam's completion. The River and Harbor Act of 1909 approved a survey of the Tallapoosa, Coosa, and Etowah Rivers to evaluate their power, navigation, and flood potential. The Corps of Engineers did not recommend that the federal government should improve those rivers for economic benefits. Their decision did not deter state and local hydroelectric developers.

Alexander City's Russell family also recognized the possibilities of the Tallapoosa River. In 1902, Benjamin Russell opened his first textile mill with eight knitting machines; the mill was the forerunner of a major international clothing manufacturing corporation. Russell was also involved in early efforts to develop the Tallapoosa River to generate hydroelectric power.

Russell and Industries Light and Power Company planned to build a dam at Buzzard Roost Shoals and built a cofferdam there. They realized that this site was upstream from the Cherokee Bluffs site and would be flooded. Russell also realized that the Cherokee Bluffs dam would be more beneficial to more people than the Buzzard Roost Shoals dam he envisioned. Martin remembered that the

> broad-minded Russell recognized the greater public benefit from the complete development of the power of the stream; thereupon a satisfactory agreement was reached with Russell for purchase of his properties and for supplying his enterprises with power. The agreement was carried out to the satisfaction of all parties, and through the years Benjamin Russell was a fast friend of the Power Company and of its officials, helpful in many of its problems.

Russell owned a vast amount of property near Cherokee Bluffs that "was essential to the complete development of Cherokee Bluffs," and he later helped Alabama Power Company officials interested in the area. Power company personnel valued industrialist Russell's knowledge of local topography and people's expectations, which guided them as they pursued development of Tallapoosa River lands. After obtaining Russell's cooperation, the power company focused on securing options to the Tallassee mills' excess river power rights.

In 1911, Captain James R. Hall of Dadeville and Henry Horne of Macon, Georgia, contacted Nora E. Miller, a respected Dadeville resident whom they considered "untiring" and "zealous" in pursuing her interests. The men told her about the "possibilities for power, latent in the Tallapoosa River." Miller had lived in the Tallapoosa County area for a long time and "knew the territory like the palm of her hand, knew every person in the county." Hall knew that Miller had "just demonstrated her splendid spirit of upbuilding by personally raising the funds to match a state appropriation for building a road from Dadeville to the historical battleground of Horseshoe Bend." She owned some of the land where the battle occurred. Considering Miller a "most valuable ally," Hall and Horne hoped she could help make "their dreams of power development come true." She loaned the men her automobile, and they "busied themselves in locating dam sites and securing options on the lands needed" in the possible basin area. Horne asked New York businessman Paul T. Brady to assist in securing funds to develop the river. Brady knew James Mitchell, a Massachusetts entrepreneur who had money and experience others lacked, and convinced him to consider damming the Tallapoosa. Mitchell visited Thomas W. Martin at the Montgomery law firm Tyson, Wilson & Martin where he was a partner. Alabama Power Company vice-president and general manager J.M. Barry commented in 1941 that

> When James Mitchell walked into the law office of Thos. W. Martin in Montgomery in November 1911, it was an historic occasion. Although probably neither man realized it at the time, it was the beginning of a relationship which was to lead to the beginning of a relationship which was to lead to the building of a great power system—a system which has been an outstanding force in the development of our State and the South.

Thomas W. Martin considered James Mitchell to be a "genius" and encouraged his interest in Cherokee Bluffs as a potential dam site. Martin later reminisced:

> An incident took place in 1911 on the banks of the Tallapoosa at what we called Cherokee Bluffs in that day; an incident which forecast the development of the hydro powers of our State. James Mitchell came by invitation of the owners of the Cherokee power site, to look things over. A stranger to the state, he had come alone. A few of us met him at Cherokee Bluffs and with him viewed the stream, visualized a great power dam, the storage of vast quantities of water and a state-wide power system. Remembering that meeting in after years, we erected a viewhouse over the spot where we talked in that eventful year of 1911.

Mitchell had driven a buggy to Cherokee Bluffs from Opelika and "up to that time had never set foot on Alabama soil." He was impressed by what he saw. Mitchell "looked at this river and these great hills attracted him." Jones said Mitchell had "vision" and during his 15-minute reflection atop Cherokee Bluffs "recognized in Cherokee the keystone to successful waterpower development in Alabama" and decided to proceed. Mitchell devoted his energy to Cherokee Bluffs and "informed himself about our State: its public policies of friendly invitation to outside capital to come in and help us develop our natural resources." Most importantly, "he made up his mind that here a mighty dam could be built to bring power and light to the public."

In 1912, Mitchell became president of the Alabama Power Company. Captain Lay told Mitchell, "I now commit to you the good name and destiny of the Alabama Power Company. May it be developed for the service of Alabama." Martin emphasized that Mitchell "did not think of the latent energy of streams as just so much electricity to be captured and sold as merchandise, rather did he visualize this force in the life of our people as affording more leisure, better education, better health and greater opportunities for employment."

Miller hosted Mitchell in her Dadeville home when he visited to survey the land that would become the dam's reservoir. She accompanied Mitchell in her Winton Six automobile, driving throughout Tallapoosa County to meet landowners. Mitchell became aware that the Tallapoosa River was not suitable for run-of-the-river power generation but

NORA MILLER. Miller guided Alabama Power Company representatives around the future Lake Martin site.

"its tremendous storage possibilities would make it possible to harness this stream in tandem with the Coosa so as to have a year-round supply of hydro-electric energy."

The power company pushed ahead to acquire land for the dam. Martin acknowledged that Russell "was one of those few who from the start saw the great boom which would come, not alone to the County but to the people of the State, from the development of its water powers." *Powergrams* noted that "Mrs. Miller secured for them [Horne and Hall] several very vital locations on the river without which the great developments contemplated could not have proceeded and also rendered other services of great value." When offered payment, Miller declared, "I want no remuneration of any kind except the consciousness of having a part in the development of Alabama." Miller became known as the "Mother of Cherokee Bluffs." Mitchell presented Miller an engraved silver trowel, saying she was to use it at the ceremony when the dam's cornerstone was laid. She protected it with velvet and eagerly awaited the future celebration where she would "lay the first trowel of cement."

Martin represented the Cherokee Bluffs owners and Alabama Power Company in dam-related litigation. He secured the legal right to develop the Lock 12 (Lay Dam) site from the state supreme court in 1912. This resulted in him being chosen as the Alabama Power Company's general counsel. Martin won the "mosquito" lawsuits for the power company, which had been sued after the Lay Dam was built. He arranged for yellow fever expert and native Alabamian General William C. Gorgas to testify that the Alabama Power Company was not liable for illnesses in the Lay Dam reservoir area. After he became Alabama Power Company vice president in 1915, Martin continued as that company's legal counsel.

By 1916, the Alabama Power Company obtained rights to build a dam at Cherokee Bluffs. The Alabama Power Company was involved in a legal dispute about the right to develop the Tallapoosa River as a public power source despite downstream property owners' objections. Representatives of the Mount Vernon-Woodberry Cotton Duck Company argued that the land the power company was condemning and seizing was not being used for public applications. The case, *Mount Vernon-Woodberry Cotton Duck Company v. Alabama Interstate Power Company*, was heard in state courts and the Alabama Supreme Court. By 1916, it reached the United States Supreme Court, which ruled that Alabama's condemnation statute was constitutional, thus validating the power company's right to pursue hydroelectric developments, including taking private property "by eminent domain." Justice Oliver Wendell Holmes made a statement on the case that has often been quoted: "To gather the streams from waste and to draw from them energy, labor without brains, and so to save mankind from toil that it can be spared, is to supply what, next to intellect, is the very foundation of all our achievements and all our welfare." Despite this court victory, immediate work at Cherokee Bluffs was delayed by World War I.

The Federal Water Power Act, passed in 1920, expanded opportunities for the Alabama Power Company to plan and build more hydroelectric power plants. That act created the Federal Power Commission to license hydroelectric developments on public lands. Mitchell had suffered a cerebral hemorrhage in June 1919 and died the next year, but his colleagues continued his work, and Martin was unanimously selected as Alabama Power Company's president. He expanded Mitchell's plans. On August 28, 1922, the Alabama Power Company applied for dam permits for Cherokee Bluffs development to the Alabama Public Service Commission and Federal Power Commission.

In 1923, Walter E. Sanford wrote a *Powergrams* article, "Tallapoosa River Development," chronicling plans for dams on that river. He said that daily gauge readings over a 26-year period measured a minimum flow of 300 cubic feet per second at Cherokee Bluffs before a dam was built. Sanford estimated this flow would increase to as high as 3,700 cubic feet per second when the dam was completed and the reservoir formed. He explained that studies recommended placing a chain of dams on the river so that water was most efficiently used. This could be achieved by placing the "dams in such locations that the reservoir of one will end at the tail water of the next above it, and in this way not lose any of the fall of the river between dams." These studies recognized that "on the Tallapoosa, because of the many suitable dam sites, only a small amount of fall will be lost between dams."

Experts advised building the chain's first dam at Cherokee Bluffs. That dam would have an approximately 150-foot "head of water acting on the turbines." The power company planned to build two dams near Tallassee below the Cherokee Bluffs dam "so as to use the entire fall of the river in this section." Power company engineers stated that the "storage water at Cherokee Bluffs and above will then be used as it passes through each of these plants to generate more power" in order to "convert the water of the Tallapoosa River into useful energy for the people of the State of Alabama and nearby states." Combined with the Tallassee Falls dam in the chain, engineers realized that "With the completion of the Cherokee Bluff's dam and the Upper Tallassee dam, the same water within the short space of eleven miles will then be used three separate times for the generation of electric power for the use of Alabama institutions."

4. Creating Lake Martin,
1923 to 1926

Work related to dam construction began at Cherokee Bluffs during 1923. The Federal Power Commission issued a 50-year license for the Cherokee Bluffs dam on June 9, 1923, and the Alabama Power Company estimated that dam construction would require at least two years. The Cherokee Bluffs Dam was the first well-documented project in the Alabama Power Company's early history. Preliminary work to prepare the Tallapoosa River basin lasted for several months. Thomas W. Martin later recalled that the "changes to be wrought in this beautiful valley by the construction of the dam at Cherokee Bluffs were to bring many problems, both human and physical." He commented that "There were some sixty thousand acres of land to be acquired, with attendant upsets in ways and places of living for many families" and "Many bridges and one hundred miles of highway were to be destroyed by the impounded waters and substitutes had to be provided at the cost of the Company." Martin also noted that "in addition to the engineering work, a mountain of legal work was necessary," including "abstracts prepared, titles examined."

From 1923 to 1926, rolling Alabama farmland and timber was transformed into a magnificent lake that created energy and opportunities. The power company was aware that most Alabamians would not realize the extensive nature of works and related costs necessary to prepare land for dam construction and flooding. For example, in February 1923, the power company hired an aerial photographer to map topographically the Tallapoosa River basin. The cameraman, flying in a Breguet biplane, photographed 500 square miles of hilly, thick timber surrounding the designated dam and reservoir site.

On the ground, University of Alabama geologist Dr. Stewart J. Lloyd and Dr. Crosby evaluated the Tallapoosa riverbed geology. In a laboratory, engineers built 1/100th scale models resembling Cherokee Bluffs to plan dam construction and possible hydrological situations, particularly flooding. Ireal Winter, head of the power company's laboratory division in the engineering department, later revealed how useful the models of the dam and riverbed were. "The Martin Dam development presented several very interesting problems which were worked out satisfactorily in the small model before the dam was constructed," Winter stated. "By the use of this model it was possible to design the spillway aprons in such manner that the destructive action of the flood water on the river bed was reduced to a minimum." The Alabama Power Company frequently consulted the model laboratory to determine how the dam would react to "unusual stresses and strains as the result of the impounding of so great a volume of water."

Surveyors staked out the future lake's perimeters where the dammed water would overflow. Land agents C.B. McGriff and Victor O. Russell, representing the Alabama Power Company's Land Department, traveled to Dadeville and contacted people who owned property, mostly farms and timber, in the designated reservoir basin in order to buy those lands. McGriff had previous experience securing rights-of-way for power company projects in Alabama and Georgia. Russell was a self-described "dirt" farmer and merchant. The July 1923 *Powergrams* stated that "Both are well acquainted with terra firma and should be able to handle their duties in an efficient manner." Dadeville resident Morgan "Dam" Jones, also a power company employee, purchased land.

But many landowners were reluctant to sell their property. They resented the power company's demands that they leave their homesteads, many of which had belonged to families for almost 100 years. People did not want to leave the houses, barns, and farm structures they had built or the rural communities where they resided. Although the power company reassured landowners that they would be equitably compensated and could buy better homes in towns, rural people did not want to exchange their property for urban lifestyles. Some people did not believe that the dam could back water up so far to cause a large, deep lake to form, so they did not think they needed to leave. Moonshiners could not publicly complain about having to abandon the "deep wooded hollows with

BIPLANE. This plane was used to map the Tallapoosa River basin prior to dam construction. An aerial view was necessary for engineers to comprehend how to develop the territory.

their clear, cold spring branches" that "afforded many excellent sites for the manufacture of this illicit product." They resented "having to break up the stills and move them to a higher elevation with less satisfactory natural facilities and making it easier for the law officers to find them was most disconcerting to the owners."

Because the power company insisted on dam construction for flood control and energy generation, residents living in the future flooded areas had no choice and were forced to leave. Commenting about property acquisition, Martin stressed that "Even if we had the right to acquire them by condemnation, we were determined to avoid that course." Some people were eager to accept the power company's money, ranging from $12 to $40 per acre, and depart because they thought the lake might cause typhoid, yellow fever, and malaria. Land agents tried to entice people to move to nearby states with offers of free trips and paid expenses while looking at properties.

Aubrey Farrow, who cleared the basin and worked at the dam, remembered that some people did not sell all of their property. "A lot of people had land on the 490 mark [the proposed lake's highest elevation] and had to sell it and move out," Farrow said. "Lots of people sold the land and sold the water right, but kept the land above the 490 mark. That's why you see a lot of these beautiful old homes around the lake." Most people relocated to Alexander City, Dadeville, Eclectic, or Tallassee and worked in the mills or local businesses. Farmers were often dissatisfied with new farm land they attempted to cultivate because it was not as rich as the reservoir's bottomlands.

The power company also identified churches and cemeteries, both white and black, in the surveyed reservoir basin. Many graves were moved to other locations after the power

RURAL CEMETERY. *Pictured here before the graves were moved, these unidentified men and young boy waited for the power company officials to discuss grave removal policies.*

company contacted relatives or representatives who approved transferring the deceased. The power company contracted Alexander City undertaker E.J. Duncan to perform this work. One relative affirmed that the "Alabama Power Company was good in this and carefully marked the removal of remains with names and numbers and metal stakes for careful exactness." Graves that could not be relocated were sealed shut with concrete slabs. This work was considered the most emotionally draining for the families and workers. Many Alabama pioneers lie buried deep beneath the waters of Lake Martin. Others remained on islands of land that were not covered by the reservoir except when extreme flooding conditions occurred.

Some people relocated houses, but most structures, including pioneers' log cabins, were destroyed. After people moved, crews burned buildings, including houses, stores, and schools. Some stone buildings could not be burned. Those structures still appeared as black rectangles beneath the lake on some maps. Some of the Central of Georgia Railroad track was relocated to higher ground.

The July 1923 *Powergrams* noted that "Work at Cherokee Bluffs Started." On June 15, Martin had "made known work is to begin immediately on a giant dam and powerhouse at Cherokee Bluffs on the Tallapoosa River which will develop 132,000 horsepower and cost approximately $10,000,000." He had also ordered work to commence at the 40,000-horsepower upper and lower Tallassee dam developments. *Powergrams* speculated that "Alabama Power Company, youngest of the great power producers, will soon be the largest in the South in the amount of electric energy generated." The magazine stated, "It is doubtful if such a stupendous plan for turning the Southern streams from waste has ever been undertaken by a corporation at one time," concluding that the "Power Company is receiving plaudits from every hand for continuing constructive work instead of resting on its great achievement in completing Mitchell Dam."

Martin emphasized that increasing Alabama's power generation capabilities was essential because other Southern power companies were not going to proceed with additional power developments. He noted that steam plants would be incapable of producing sufficient energy. Martin hoped that "this development will not only improve the service throughout the power system of the Company, but will make available a large additional volume of power." He envisioned the Cherokee Bluffs dam "will enable the Company to further meet the industrial needs of the State as well as supplying lighting and power service in many communities which have requested service from the Company." He stressed that the availability of ample hydroelectric power would entice industries to select Alabama for manufacturing sites instead of other states.

Powergrams commented that Oscar G. Thurlow, the chief engineer of the Cherokee Bluffs project, was pursuing a "distinct departure from the plan usually followed in works of its kind in this section." For example, the dam's power house would be built on the downstream side. The three 44,000-horsepower units would be the largest at dams in the United States and second in size only to the units in Canada opposite Niagara Falls. Thurlow's expertise included designing spillways specifically for the Tallapoosa River dams. Readers learned that, at 120 feet high, the Cherokee Bluffs dam would be the South's tallest. The dam would stretch 800 feet across the Tallapoosa River and consist of 200,000 yards of concrete. According to company policy, only materials from Alabama

THE MARTIN DAM. This sketch shows the proposed Martin Dam, powerhouse, and reservoir. The artist realistically depicted the dam structures, although the actual physical appearance of the lake that formed and its surroundings differ.

resources would be utilized. Engineers initially thought the lake created by the dam would extend across a 25,000-acre area and hold 25 billion cubic feet of water. When completely filled, the lake would be Alabama's largest body of water.

Preparations for dam construction included clearing the reservoir basin and developing infrastructure to support laborers. Because the power company contracted the Dixie Construction Company for dam building, that business provided most of the workers at Cherokee Bluffs. Mule-drawn drays delivered early loads of construction equipment. A camp to shelter at least 3,000 people was the first priority. The construction camp would house a maximum of 1,800 employees and their families. The Alabama Power Company envisioned building "a modern city in the wilderness" and promised that "all of the necessaries and many of the luxuries usually found in a city will be provided." Alabama Power Company officials said that the camp would be larger than Alexander City at that time. They assured workers that the Cherokee Bluffs community would be better than the Mitchell Dam camp based on the company's experiences there.

The power company was especially concerned about people's comfort and health in the camp. More than 100 carpenters began building the camp before starting dam construction work. The camp had a total of 250 buildings composed of 1 million feet of lumber. Described as a "model miniature city," the campsite had streets and an office and warehouses. Features included electricity, water, and sewer services. The construction camp kitchen had electrical appliances. A pumping plant was built to "elevate river water to the highest knoll on the reservation where it will be purified for personal use by adequate filtration and chlorination." *Powergrams* reported that this water was "periodically analyzed for impurities of any kind and steps are taken to prevent the slightest trace of disease-bearing bacteria." The power company's magazine noted that the "final product of this process is actually so pure that persons who drink it are liable to suffer for a while from digestive derangements before their systems become accustomed to the absence of impurities."

Camp buildings included bathhouses and housing, consisting of segregated bunk houses and huts for white, Mexican, and black laborers. Other camp structures were a commissary, school, dining hall, recreation hall, and barber shop. Camp residents could attend churches and watch motion pictures at the site. By November, a high-tension transmission line was strung from the Upper Tallassee dam to Cherokee Bluffs. Cherokee Bluffs was also connected to the Tallassee Falls Bell telephone system so personnel in the power company's Birmingham offices could contact Cherokee Bluffs directly.

The power company was especially concerned with the health and safety of dam workers and their families. *Powergrams* reported that "There has been installed at the Cherokee Bluffs camp a hospital containing the most modern and complete equipment obtainable and supervised by a competent medical force, thoroughly versed in the Company's methods of disease prevention." Because mosquitoes posed a malaria threat, each employee underwent a complete physical examination. Anyone with "malaria in his blood as revealed in a laboratory analysis" was not employed. Health workers also evaluated the extent of malaria in area residents. At first, their efforts focused on stopping transmission of malaria from inhabitants to employees clearing the basin. They examined and took blood samples from all residents and collected local malaria histories. *Powergrams* explained that people diagnosed with malaria were treated with quinine. Employees were regularly dosed with quinine.

MESS HALL AND HOUSING AT CHEROKEE BLUFFS. Workers are shown using lumber harvested from the reservoir to construct the buildings.

In the construction camp, screens were placed on the houses, and the "woods and thickets for a radius of a mile from the camp are sprinkled constantly with heavy oil to halt mosquito breeding."

Because Cherokee Bluffs was such a remote and rugged site, the camp hospital was equipped to handle emergencies since patients could not be transported quickly to area hospitals. Electrical sterilizers for surgical tools and X-ray machines were transferred from the Mitchell Dam hospital. Surgeons, a dentist, and white and black nurses tended all employees and family members. Wards were segregated, and private rooms were available for female patients or workers suffering extreme conditions. Several babies were born at the camp hospital. The hospital had a laboratory for specimen analysis, laundry, and an electrified kitchen. Sadly, however, some workers were killed when trees fell on them or they fell into the concrete.

The Alabama Power Company wanted to prevent typhoid fever from occurring at Cherokee Bluffs and its other dam projects, and "This dread disease is guarded against in every possible way, not only in purifying the water supply but in active work in fly-control, food inspections, garbage disposal and the like."

Several of the "Dam Builders" in charge had worked at the recently completed Mitchell Dam on the Coosa River. L.V. Branch was the division engineer in charge of Cherokee Bluffs construction, and he had worked on five dams before the Cherokee Bluffs project, including a dam in Puerto Rico where he had met Thurlow. C.C. Davis served as superintendent of construction at Mitchell before being assigned the same position at Cherokee Bluffs. L.G. Warren was the assistant superintendent in charge of engineering.

EXTERIOR OF MESS HALL AND HOUSING AT CHEROKEE BLUFFS. These hungry men are patiently waiting for the mess hall to open so they can eat.

CHEROKEE BLUFFS. *These pictures show the railroad, sawmill, hospital, and quarry. The Cherokee Bluff site provided an ample source of materials to build the dam and affiliated structures.*

John Scott was in charge of supplies and materials at Cherokee Bluffs. R.C. Craven was the master mechanic, and R.C. Porter was the resident engineer overseeing the railroad construction. Major W.S. Winn was the project engineer who directed the river survey and water power engineering. Robert Klein was employed as office manager. "With this array of veterans on the job," *Powergrams* stated, "it is felt that the huge task of adding Cherokee Bluffs to the Company's list of generating plants on schedule time is an assured certainty."

Reservoir preparation was intensive. The 1920 Federal Water Power Act declared that "all trees whose tops will protrude above water must be felled and the shore line must be absolutely cleared for a distance of 20 feet above low water level, to permit wave action and eliminate mosquito breeding places." The power company acknowledged that a "large item of expense is the necessity for clearing the land before it is flooded as a health measure, to make the reservoir navigable and sightly and to remove obstructions which might impede the operation of the water wheels." *Powergrams* reported that the "clearing of all trees above a certain area in the Martin Dam Basin was a herculean task. Trees that would extend above the low water level were felled and tied down with strands of wire. The area between the low water level and the high water level was completely cleared."

For the Cherokee Bluffs project, power company officials wanted to surpass federal requirements and "resolved to make this lake as clear as possible by removing absolutely all vegetation before the waters are impounded." The company wanted all trees and brush stripped from the area where the lake would form. "In order to make this reservoir safely navigable, healthful and beautiful and to minimize likelihood of the water

DAM CONSTRUCTION. These scenes at Cherokee Bluffs show different phases and areas involved in building the dam. Groups of specialized workers were spread out at different sites.

wheels becoming clogged by timber and underbrush," *Powergrams* explained, "The Alabama Power Company is spending approximately $1,000,000 in making it as clean as a kitchen floor."

Various clearing methods involved only removing the largest trees and cutting smaller trees so they fell bent close to the ground and were still connected to their stumps. In that clearing system, the river would wash away underbrush as its level rose. The Alabama Power Company thought this method would be compatible with power generation, but would result in debris collecting in spillways. The remaining tree trunks, stumps, and brush might interfere with navigation, and water could become unhealthy and polluted with "carboniferous matter." Explaining that other forms of clearing would be three times costlier, the periodical stated that the "most approved methods are used and added to those hitherto employed include a number of improvements invented by Power Company engineers and devised to meet the specific problems encountered."

The power company promoted its clearing method because, in contrast to previous dam reservoir projects, it wanted Cherokee Bluffs to be "as clean of permanently lodged matter as any body of water, natural or artificial, in existence and as such will be an asset to the transportation and recreation facilities of the State." *Powergrams* reminded readers that the reservoir would also serve as a "safeguard against floods, a boon to all year navigation of the Alabama River to the Gulf of Mexico and a continuous source of cheap and reliable hydro-electric energy."

According to the power company's description, the "lake basin covers a goodly section of the counties of Coosa, Tallapoosa and Elmore," and "For the most part, the land which will be inundated by the reservoir is barren or covered with second growth timber with an occasional remotely situated farm." The power company realized that "much of the territory is clothed in virgin woods or second-growth timber of great enough age to make good lumber." Officials decided that "rather than burn this, as the underbrush is treated, several sawmills have been set up and are engaged in sawing the trees into lumber, which will be used in constructing the dam and devoted to other useful purposes."

A three-step clearing procedure of cutting, skidding, and burning stripped the ground of all vegetation and debris. H.T. Sims supervised clearing from an Alexander City headquarters. H.C. Lee monitored work in the basin's eastern half, and Frank Higgins oversaw the western part of the basin. S.S. Hunter was in charge of all field engineering. E.T. Davis, of the power company's Land Department, coordinated land purchases and clearing.

The power company hired approximately 1,000 reservoir clearers. *Powergrams* noted that it is "impossible for men whose work covers 40,000 acres to maintain established headquarters. Accordingly, the strippers live in camps which are moved from place to place as the swathe of forest is cut about them." Clearing began in northeast Elmore County near where Kowaliga Creek entered the Tallapoosa River. The men set up portable shelters and equipment "in the midst of a veritable forest of heavy timber." Camp cooks, such as one cook named Mayo, fed the clearing crews. The workers transformed the "silent retreat of wild birds and animals into a hive of industry."

The men worked as sawyers, skidders, and burners, and the "different units are complete in themselves and are spaced at wide distances from each other, so that the reducing of the forest will be accomplished uniformly." The sawyers used axes and cross-cut saws to cut all trees and brush in the basin. Logging teams removed trees identified as being large enough and of a suitable quality to be made into lumber. Workers built 25 sawmills supervised by superintendent Charles E. Gulledge to process choice timber harvested from the reservoir site to use as lumber for aspects of dam and camp

CLEARING THE CHEROKEE BASIN. Cutting, skidder, and burning crews cleared the area prior to dam construction.

construction. In some places, extremely large trees were chained or tied to the ground to prevent them from floating to the surface of the flooded reservoir. Inferior wood was often burned without being cut to save time.

Skidding crews followed the sawyers to pile up remaining trunks, limbs, and debris. Workers used tractors adapted with rollers, drums, and cables to move woody materials efficiently. These machines were called skidders. *Powergrams* explained how the skidding process worked: "The front end of the skidder is anchored to a stump and the cable unreeled and hitched to the fallen trees and piles of underbrush so that when its burden is drawn in it may be deposited where desired." During the next step the long "cable is again unwound and the process repeated until the ground within its radius is barren." The magazine noted that the machinery could quickly clear an area. "As a rule, a movable pulley, through which the cable is passed, is affixed to a stump in the center of the space to be cleared and this stump is the central point of the pile," *Powergrams* described. "This makes it possible for the skidder to remain in the same position and clear from the pile of brushwood which it collects." Although mechanized pile accumulation was costly, power company officials decided the expense was merited because skidders were more efficient than mule-powered equipment. Burners followed the skidders and checked for any overlooked debris. The burners waited until the piles were dry before they burned them.

Such measures helped minimize the future lake's mosquito breeding habitats. Alabama Power Company engineer F.C. Weiss and state health officer Dr. S.W. Welch met with state and local public health personnel to address how to prevent mosquitoes from surviving and reproducing at the impounded lake that would be created by the

BEGINNING OF COFFERDAM CRIB. Also shown here are grading land for the railroad and a noon break. Both men and mules worked hard at transforming the landscape.

COFFERDAM IN TALLAPOOSA RIVER. Workers sealed off an area in the river to pump out water and expose the riverbed in order to build the dam's foundation.

Cherokee Bluffs dam. They decided to use the same effective method as Weiss and the State Board of Health had developed for mosquito control at Mitchell Dam. That technique called for digging small ponds along the streams in the area that was to be flooded. The ponds were stocked with several hundred top minnows (*Gambusia*), which ate mosquito larvae, commonly called "wiggle-tail." The minnows multiplied to a population of several hundred thousand by the time lake water rose high enough to free them from the ponds. They could swim easily in shallow areas near shorelines where mosquitoes laid their larvae. The minnows killed mosquitoes before they were old enough to transmit malaria to people.

"Such rapid progress is being made at Cherokee Bluffs that it is almost impossible to give accurate news as to progress there," the August 1923 *Powergrams* explained, "for the reason that by the time a article finds its way into print, work has gained so greatly in momentum that the very face of the earth has been altered." Four hundred employees were working at the Cherokee Bluffs dam site by September 1943, and work accelerated that autumn. "Surveying forces have completed their work at the Russell site on the Tallapoosa River and are being moved away this week," *Powergrams* announced in October. The periodical noted, "Their examination of the site proved it to be very satisfactory in every way for the location of a dam."

In addition to clearing the reservoir basin, the power company planned to build a company railway to move supplies shipped from Birmingham and Montgomery from the main railroad lines to the dam construction site. On July 20, the Alabama Power Company contracted with C.B. Cox from Clanton to grade 70,000 yards for the company's railroad right-of-way. The company's railway would extend from Asberry Station where the

FLOODGATES UNDER CONSTRUCTION. The locomotive on the tracks in the center of the picture reveals the enormous size of the dam.

Birmingham and Southeastern Railroad stopped at a terminal and could switch cars to the power company's yards at dam site at Cherokee Bluffs. At previous dam projects, the power company had relied solely on railroads to transport heavy supplies and construction equipment and determined that a company railroad would be more convenient.

Cox sent mule teams and a steam shovel to begin grading on July 31. The Warrior Steam plant sent another steam shovel to the site. Workers also began work on railway culverts and bridges, and trestles were placed over streams and Channohatchie Creek. Workers made forms, poured 14 concrete piers, and erected steel girders to build a 625-foot railroad bridge spanning the Tallapoosa River to transport construction materials and machinery to the dam site. The railroad was ready by January 10, 1924. Locomotives pulled flatcars, carrying derricks to Cherokee Bluffs. With this technology, *Powergrams* assured readers, "Things will then begin to hum at Cherokee and another big hydro-electric plant will begin to materialize." During construction, the Cherokee Bluffs railroad transported 1,500 cars of cement, 8,000 of gravel, 4,000 of sand, 2,000 of plumbstone, 750 of "miscellaneous merchandise," 250 of coal, 100 of machinery, 100 of lumber, and 100 of ice and groceries.

Meanwhile, workers placed timbers in the riverbed to form cofferdam cribs. Every day, the cofferdams extended further from the bank to reach across the river channel. By December 1923, Coffer No. 1 was "200 feet long by 300 feet up and down stream" and covered "an area in the west half of the river bed." *Powergrams* noted that "This coffer can withstand a flood of 34,000 cubic feet per second without being overtopped. The maximum height where the coffer crosses the deep channel is 33 feet."

The completion of the cofferdams enabled excavation of the nearby dam site to begin. Water was pumped from the cofferdams "to bare the river channel for the foundation work." *Powergrams* noted that "Two centrifugal pumps of large capacity, which were already installed, are now rendering day and night duty at this task." In order to advance work, the "cofferdams will be tracked and the locomotives and cars will carry the material from the mixers to within reach of the derricks, which will be placed at such points that every section of the dam will be within reach of their booms."

After the area was pumped dry, workers blasted parts of the dam site. The excavation site produced at least 10,000 cubic yards of rock for construction of dam and power house foundations. An adjacent plumbstone quarry provided huge stone block that laborers loaded on flatcars with derricks. "The work of stripping and developing the face of the quarry has been started," *Powergrams* reported in February 1924, stating "It is planned to take the rock out in shallow layers with light shots to avoid breaking it any more than necessary." The quarry's rubble was collected for use in concrete work. Warehouses held and processed gravel and sand shipped from the Montgomery Sand and Gravel Company. That company extracted gravel and sand from pits at Mt. Meigs, then shipped those materials by railroad to Cherokee Bluffs. Dam workers used mixers to combine supplies to produce concrete. Seaborn Adamson recalled that he "operated a train that pulled a transformer wagon; hauled cement, logs and rocks from the rock quarry to the crusher; and put lights down so the night shift could work." He joked, "I think I hauled about a million-and-a-half yards of cement."

Workers also began placing creosoted poles with galvanized hardware and insulators and stringing copper wire cables for future transmissions. "The section of the line from Mitchell Dam to Cherokee Bluffs is important, not only on account of supplying power for distribution at North Auburn and for construction of the Cherokee Bluffs plant," S.S. Simpson stated in March 1924, "but also because branch lines have been built from Cherokee Bluffs that will distribute power from Mitchell Dam to Tallassee, Notasulga, Union Springs and Montgomery." Work was delayed by constant rainfall and an unusually severe winter which made roads sloppy. "According to reports received from [power

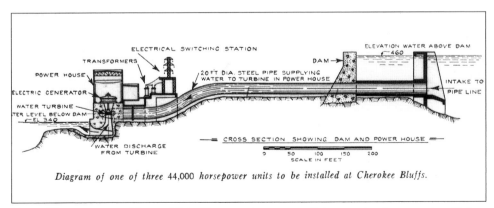

Diagram of one of three 44,000 horsepower units to be installed at Cherokee Bluffs.

DAM HORSEPOWER UNIT. *This diagram shows one of three units that was installed at Cherokee Bluffs.*

company employee] Lawrence Lineberry," *Powergrams* reported, "the road to Cherokee Bluffs is pretty rough." Flood waters disrupted dam construction in early 1925. While the dam was being constructed, workers endured eight "major floods that caused setbacks, destroyed equipment, and hindered progress. As the spillway section was constructed, five bays were left unconstructed until the last in order to leave a place for the river to pass through."

Local people often watched construction at Cherokee Bluffs. Families picnicked as they observed the dam builders. Olivia T. Sheppard recalled accompanying her father Chilton W. Thomas when he took photographs of the construction. *Powergrams* wrote that Nora E. Miller "had seen the cofferdams thrust into the stream, had heard the clatter of the drills digging the monolith's foundations in the bed of the Tallapoosa and had seen the Cherokee wilderness swarming with the hordes of men about to 'gather the stream from waste.' " Dam construction progressed as components were built and put in place.

In June 1925, people spread rumors that work on the Cherokee Bluffs project would be stopped. Martin assured Alabamians that construction was continuing and that the dam and lake would be ready for use by late 1926. *Powergrams* declared that "Completion of the storage plant will provide the greatest artificial lake in the world, with an impounding capacity of 530 billion gallons of water." Previously, Roosevelt Dam Reservoir, holding 420 billion gallons, was the largest artificial water body. The magazine also said that the "lake will have an area much greater than the City of Birmingham, including all suburbs, with a shore line of 700 miles and covering 40,000 acres of farm and forest land in Tallapoosa, Coosa and Elmore Counties."

GOVERNOR WILLIAM W. BRANDON. *Brandon spoke at the 1925 cornerstone laying ceremony at Cherokee Bluffs.*

RUSSELL MILLS BAND. Hailing from Alexander City, this uniformed band played at the cornerstone ceremony.

During the summer, manufacturers submitted bids to install 45,000-horsepower hydraulic turbine-driven generators at Cherokee Bluffs. Martin stated that the Cherokee Bluffs dam would be connected with other company plants to boost power system resources and expand energy access. He was interested in extending electricity, especially to rural communities such as the Cherokee Bluffs area. Martin stressed that the "farmers are, perhaps, as much or more interested in this work than any other citizens of the State, since industrial growth will furnish them local customers and consumers for their products." Agriculturists were pleased by Martin's attention. In addition to expanding electrical access, farmers were aware that the lake would result in the farmland south of it becoming "frost-proof." The large water body would influence the area's climate, making it possible for farmers to grow commercial fruit crops, especially grapes, apples, and pears.

Because the Tallapoosa River fluctuated seasonally, the Cherokee Bluffs dam was built tall so that "With the higher dam forming a vast reservoir, it is possible to conserve the water during the wet seasons and release it through the turbines in constant volume throughout the year." Cherokee Bluffs would aid in reducing the "necessity for excessive reserve steam power" by "bearing much of the load of 'run-of-river' plants during low water periods." The lake would guard rich soil south of the dam from floods and assure that the Alabama River would be navigable to the Gulf of Mexico. "Not the least of the advantages which will be provided by the Cherokee Bluffs plant," *Powergrams* insisted, "will be the opening to transportation of a great area which hitherto has been connected with the railroads by poor roads or has been barren and unproductive by reason of no roads at all."

The August 1925 *Powergrams* printed an editorial, "The Cherokee Bluffs Lake," predicting that the lake would become Alabama's significant landmark. The magazine suggested the lake's tourist potential because "aside from serving as a storage bin for the water which will keep the generators in action, the lake will be Alabama's largest single advertising medium, which has already been the subject of many articles published in national periodicals." Commenting that "Practically every State in the Union has its own peculiar attraction," such as Georgia's Stone Mountain, *Powergrams* declared that "Cherokee Bluffs Lake will be Alabama's."

The formal Cherokee Bluffs cornerstone laying ceremony was celebrated on November 7, 1925, and the November 1925 *Powergrams* was devoted to the coverage of the celebration. That publication reported that the Cherokee Bluffs dam had cost $13 million to build. Traveling by specially chartered trains and automobiles, several thousand people attended the event. They were "seated in the great natural amphitheater formed by the bluffs and foothills" to listen to speeches. Flags and patriotic banners and bunting decorated the speakers platform. An "elaborate barbecue" was "served from scores of tables near the dam site."

Alabama Power Company president Martin served as master of ceremonies, and John R. Hobbs, from Birmingham, presented the invocation and benediction. The Russell Mills Band played music. Honored political guests included Alabama governor William W. Brandon, Senators J. Thomas Heflin and John Craft, and Congressmen John McDuffie and W.B. Bowling. Other dignitaries present were A.G. Patterson, president of the Alabama Public Service Commission, and John A. Rogers, chairman of the state highway commission. A "who's who" of Southern railroad, iron, and lumber executives, bank officials, mayors, and civic leaders also attended.

The program consisted primarily of oratory, and "all of the speeches were made through amplifiers which made them audible as far as the crowd stretched up the hills." Martin addressed the audience, reminding them of local and technological history. He emphasized that the "State of Alabama has been blessed by nature in many ways. Its great waterpowers in the hill sections are being developed to meet the ever-growing demand of factory, farm and city dweller." He stressed the need for "the impounding and use of nature's floods to replace, at least in part, the use of coal in operating reserve steam plants," explaining that "This is a greater advance in the conservation of water resources than any step thus far taken in the history of power development in the South."

But Martin also warned that the "water resources of our State are limited and will practically all be developed within the lifetime of many in this gathering." He remarked that public officials and electrical company representatives must cooperate to achieve efficient energy generation. Reminiscing about how the Alabama Power Company acquired the Cherokee Bluffs property, Martin remarked that "Many problems have been encountered in its construction over a period of several years; but they will shortly be overcome." He promised that the Cherokee Bluffs dam was being built to generate and transmit power "to the four corners of the State" with surpluses being shared with southern states.

Martin asserted that the "continued progress of our State consists in lifting the burdens of drudgery from the shoulders of man to the tireless shoulders of the dynamo" because "Every loafing stream is loafing at the public expense and every added kilowatt of power means less work for someone, more freedom and a richer chance for life." Speaking for the Alabama Power Company, Martin concluded that "We today dedicate the [Cherokee Bluffs] development to the public service and renew our determination to render a greater service to all sections of our State, whether city or rural community, factory or fireside."

Governor Brandon guaranteed "official sanction and approval to the efforts of the greatest developer of Alabama's natural resources, the Alabama Power Company." He promised that "As long as I am Governor I shall do all in my power, by law or otherwise, to encourage capital to come and help us develop." Referring to journalists' criticism, Brandon asserted, "If power development means the inundation of State lands, I shall give permission, and don't you pay any attention to the newspapers which condemn me for it."

Alabama Public Service Commission president Patterson discussed the history of hydroelectric power. He praised the Alabama Power Company for developing "an organization of engineers and builders of experience and ability, both necessary in the great work of constructing dams and power houses and developing markets for your product." Based on the power company's proficiency, Patterson stated that "It is now practical to harness the flow of this great stream and to substitute it for steam power." He told listeners that the Tallapoosa River was a "resource that for centuries has been going to waste, but when finally developed and transmitted to market, if sold at current prices, would yield an annual gross income of approximately $9,000,000 per year." Patterson encouraged Alabamians to continue supporting the power company's efforts at Cherokee Bluffs.

Senator Heflin recalled learning to swim in the Tallapoosa River. He referred to the "magic valley of the Tallapoosa . . . turning water into light."

LAYING THE DAM'S CORNERSTONE. *Alabama Governor William W. Brandon, Thomas W. Martin, and James Curtis Lovelace are gathered here while Lovelace used the trowel that James Mitchell gave Nora Miller.*

LAKE MARTIN

is part of the equipment necessary to produce power to turn the wheels of industry, afford employment to thousands of Alabamians, and create new wealth and opportunity in Alabama.

By reason of being able to supply current, the Alabama Power Company has been the means of bringing many new industries to the State.

Since January 1, 1926, this company has located 25 major industries in Alabama, with an aggregate annual payroll of $7,500,000. It is steadily at work bringing others. This huge lake and dam guarantee additional quantities of power, and this means many more industries, many more payrolls, more profitable employment for Alabamians, more wealth to furnish tax money for schools, more opportunities for the citizens of this State.

And additionally, if this lake proves a source of pleasure and healthful recreation to our fellow citizens, The Company is delighted for them to so make use of it, under the rules of good sportsmanship and conservation.

Alabama Power Company

THOMAS W. MARTIN, President

ALABAMA POWER COMPANY STATEMENT. These words appeared in the Alabama Sportsman. *The Alabama Power Company often publicly promoted how the Cherokee Bluffs dam and lake would benefit all Alabamians.*

James Curtis Lovelace, a cousin of Nora Miller's husband, used her trowel to smooth the concrete in the Cherokee Bluffs cornerstone. The "Mother of Cherokee Bluffs" had died on June 19, 1924, and in her will directed Lovelace, whom she had considered to be like a grandson, to assume her ceremonial role with the trowel. Lovelace had worked clearing the reservoir basin, carrying a good luck charm Miller had brought him from India. He paid tribute to his aunt when he spoke. "The Cherokee Bluffs Dam must ever take first place among the engineering achievements of the age," Lovelace said. "The raging, turbid torrents of flood-time which have hitherto surged themselves seaward through this narrow gorge, accomplishing nothing but destruction, will henceforth contribute their force to the service of man." Lovelace applauded the Cherokee Bluffs dam's "conservation of the flood-time flow, thus turning to useful account that which has always been worse than waste."

Benjamin Russell spoke on behalf of Tallapoosa County residents. "Mine is a peculiar feeling for old Tallapoose [sic] County," he said. "My grandfather settled in Tallapoosa while the Indians still roamed these hills. My parents lived and died and are buried in Tallapoosa." Russell noted that he was proud of the Tallapoosa River area where he had lived his entire life. He stated:

> I am glad that nature has made it possible for Tallapoosa County to share in providing the setting for this great giant, the foundation of which is embedded in, and the wings of which are to be tied into the solid granite of Tallapoosa and Elmore domain.

> I am not unmindful of the fact that upon Tallapoosa soil, back of this giant dam, will rest the larger part of the enormous body of water necessary to be impounded to make of this an enterprise capable of serving this and other sections in time of water distress. This means the loss to Tallapoosa County of large acreage from cultivation and yield but I firmly believe that under the changed conditions, attentiveness on our part will make for better advantages and more opportunities for Tallapoosa County than heretofore existed.

Russell praised the Alabama Power Company because it "takes the waters of the Tallapoosa which have heretofore gone to waste and gathers it together for the use and benefit and pleasure of thousands of people in this as other sections of our common country." He promised that "we of Tallapoosa County, bespeaking the friendly co-operation of your Company, will diligently strive to move forward with you to our mutual gain and understanding."

Representing Elmore County, Adolphe Hohenberg, a Wetumpka banker, asserted that the Cherokee Bluffs dam and lake would benefit local areas. People could expect improved schools, roads, and agriculture without paying increased taxes. Hohenberg said that area communities would benefit from money invested in businesses during the dam's construction phase which was, in his opinion, a "distinct local advantage." He optimistically told the crowd that "waterpower renews itself from day to day and will continue to do so as long as the sun shines and the rain falls."

Henry C. Jones, a pioneer hydroelectric power developer, narrated his early experiences with attracting investors to the Cherokee Bluffs site and devising structural plans. Commenting on the dam in progress, Jones noted, "When completed the shore line of the pond water surface will measure a distance greater than that from Montgomery to Houston, Texas, or from Montgomery to Cincinnati." He commented that the impounded water would be at least 100 billion gallons more than the reservoir of the Roosevelt Dam. Jones said that "It is with great satisfaction that its inception, 26 years ago, is on the way to realization—that this giant is to become the servant of the people."

Powergrams printed Morgan D. Jones's "Apostrophe to the Tallapoosa," an ode written for the cornerstone ceremony. The cornerstone preserved artifacts recording the dam's creation. When gathering materials for the Cherokee Bluffs dam cornerstone, Alabama Power Company representatives chose to entomb copies of the *Birmingham News*, *Powergrams*, news clippings, an Alabama history book, Alabama Department of Archives and History publications, a Confederate Memorial half-dollar, speeches and the program for the cornerstone ceremony, and items chronicling the Cherokee Bluffs site development in a sealed lead box. The cornerstone's photographs were made with inks and papers designed for extended preservation.

Newspaper coverage supported the Cherokee Bluffs project. The *Mobile Register* commented that the dam "will be a substantial contribution to Mobile's position as a seaport, though the two projects at first thought might seem to have little in common." After the dam was completed, the paper said that the "flood contribution of the Tallapoosa to the Alabama will be smaller, while the continuous release of stored waters will swell the Alabama's current in periods that would otherwise be marked by low waters." The

Alabama River would be consistently at least 4 feet deep, and barge and boat traffic between Mobile and Montgomery could travel uninterrupted.

The *Florence Herald* proclaimed Mitchell and Miller "builders for posterity." That paper announced that "As a symbol of a lofty vision, now about to become a majestic reality, the little trowel will be preserved as a memento of the dedication to the public service of the mightiest works of man." The Cherokee Bluffs trowel was later donated to the Alabama Department of Archives and History.

The *Birmingham Age-Herald*'s coverage foresaw the entertainment possibilities at Lake Martin, suggesting that the "recreational values of such a large inland body of water as the lake at Cherokee Bluffs will be very great. As a spectacle for tourists it will likewise be an asset. As a fish preserve it will assist in the program of conservation."

On June 9, 1926, workers closed the dam's gates. Gradually, the Tallapoosa River backed up into its tributaries and filled the reservoir basin. *Powergrams* noted, "Early in June 1926 the construction work of the dam had advanced to such an extent that the lake was 60 feet deep [in places], backing up the water five miles." During the next months, people watched as "every stump hole was filled" with water, stained red from eroded clay. The lake covered stagecoach routes, turpentine farms, and the remains of Creek villages. Families painfully saw their homeplaces engulfed. Farmers witnessed their fields disappear. Frank Farrow recalled, "I watched the water cover up the corn stalks, and

KOWALIGA CREEK HIGHWAY BRIDGE. *This picture shows piers under construction for the highway bridge prior to the reservoir filling.*

watermelons float off." Generations of memories vanished as home sites were submerged. Places like Susanna exist only in memories and in the ghost towns beneath the surface of the lake.

As creeks became inundated, malaria control efforts intensified. L.C. Sims supervised this work, which was considered one of the largest anti-malaria projects in the South. The "Mosquito Fleet" sprayed Lake Martin's shores from "daylight until dark." Crews used 20 motor boats with high-pressure air tanks to spray oil. Filling stations on shores and a barge replenished sprayers' oil and gasoline. *Powergrams* stated that "people living within one mile of the back water of the lake and in the basin yet unflooded were given 50,000 five-grain quinine capsules." Several hundred bed nets were also distributed along with insecticide sprayers. Furthermore, the magazine acknowledged that the Alabama State Board of Health personnel "were of the greatest help in solving the most difficult problems which arose with the elevation of the water in the Lake."

The Alabama Power Company board of directors passed a resolution at its annual meeting on June 16, 1926, officially naming the Cherokee Bluffs dam and reservoir. The board acknowledged that the "successful initiation and completion of the construction of this great project as well as other projects of the Company dedicated to the public service, has been in so large a measure due to the vision, initiative, courage and untiring efforts of Thos. W. Martin." As a result, the board announced, "Now, therefore, be it resolved, that said development hereafter be named and designated as 'Martin Dam' and that the great body of water to be formed thereby be named and designated as 'Lake Martin.' "

The front page of the September 5, 1926, *New York Times* announced "Big Power Project in Test Operation." The article summarized information the Alabama Power Company had already released. The *Times* commented that "Construction of the dam was carried on in rapid time," noting that the "first electric current was generated late last August." The New York paper provided some details not widely reported in other periodicals, including the fact that 300,000 cubic yards of stone and dirt had been excavated and "At the peak of construction, the average number of men employed daily was 2,749 and the daily payroll was estimated at $12,000." The article listed the dams whose reservoir capacities the Cherokee Bluff lake would surpass. The North American dams and reservoirs were Roosevelt Dam, Muscle Shoals Dam, Ashokan and Kensico Reservoirs, and Hetchy Dam. The *New York Times* stated that Martin Dam would supply power to both Birmingham and Atlanta and "more than 300 communities connected by transmission lines in Georgia, Alabama and Mississippi."

By October 1926, Martin Dam began testing its machinery for anticipated operation. The October 1926 *Powergrams* announced that the "fame of Martin Lake has already gone around the world, as the extracts from newspapers everywhere testify." The magazine printed the article "An Artificial Giant Lake" from the June 4, 1926, *Frankfurter Zeitung* published at Frankfort-on-the-Oder, Germany. The German newspaper reported that the new Tallapoosa River lake was the largest artificial lake in the world. The *Frankfurter Zeitung* humorously remarked that the "most astonishing thing of all is that the giant plant has the name Cherokee Bluffs, but it is no bluff at all, for it will be put in operation at the end of this year."

Construction of the Kowaliga Creek Highway Bridge was a related Martin dam and lake project. Engineers realized that Kowaliga Creek, which was the river's main tributary, would back up with high water because of its proximity to the dam. Because the Alexander City-Tallassee road bridge would be flooded, the Alabama Power Company accepted responsibility to provide alternative transportation. Discussing possibilities with Elmore County authorities, power company officials ruled out a ferry service across the narrow part of the reservoir. Engineers designed a highway bridge that the Alabama State Highway Department approved.

The Dixie Construction Company began bridge work on November 15, 1925, and continued through the winter. While that land was still dry before the reservoir began to fill completely, workers erected concrete bridge piers over Kowaliga Creek and the adjacent ground. Having observed early bridge construction, a *Powergrams* reporter said the "concrete piers and timber structures were erected mainly in open fields through which flowed a steam which appears ridiculously small in comparison with the long bridge that spans it." Compared to other bridge construction projects, "bridge engineers did not have to contend with caisons, cofferdams and troublesome water conditions in order to place the foundations."

After the piers and trestle were put in place for the 2,600-foot-long, 100-foot-high bridge, engineers waited for the reservoir to fill. When the water rose, engineers planned to use a 90-foot barge and gasoline-powered tow boat built at the dam to float steel girders from the dam to the bridge piers. Concrete forms for the girder section floor were also made. The Virginia Bridge and Iron Works in Birmingham had manufactured the girders, then transported them in pairs on three flat railcars coupled together to the dam where they awaited final bridge assembly. Master rigger Frank Wright, who had directed the placement of the 23-foot-tall bronze statue "Electra" on the Alabama Power Company building, riveted the spans and placed them on the dam's earthen dyke while waiting for water level to rise.

The Alabama Power Company declared the Cherokee Bluffs dam completed and in service on December 31, 1926. Some sources cite the next day, January 1, 1927, as the finish date. Construction costs had totaled $20 million. Robert D. Dawkins was selected to serve as the first Martin Dam superintendent. Within months, the dam backed up the Tallapoosa River, and Lake Martin was born.

5. Camps, Colonies, and Cabins: 1927 through the 1940s

Beginning in June 1926, local residents had watched the reservoir gradually fill with dammed river water and rainfall. Referred to as Cherokee Bluffs Lake and Martin's Lake, the early lake often was called the backwater by locals. Olivia Thomas Sheppard remembered, "When the backwaters came up, the main spring used for the house was covered, and we had to use the other two springs for washing and household use." She recalled fishing with cane poles and worms she found in the garden. Initially, the lake was muddy, clearing near Kowaliga and Blue Creek first. Cecil G. Duffee Jr. recalled that the "water in Lake Martin was always a muddy brown. We swam in it, but it was not a blue water lake under any imaginations. However it made a big impression on me and my friends." Suzelle Hare McGee remembered how anyone who swam came out coated in mud.

To supplement catfish in the river, the power company's Oxford Fish Hatchery stocked the lake with bass and bream to increase the new lake's fish population. The August-September 1926 *Alabama Sportsman* said that the "lake will be protected from fishing, as far as possible, for at least three years, in order to give the brood fish a chance to propagate." That magazine suggested that "Taken with what supply will come in from the Tallapoosa, the prospects are good that in four years there will be excellent fishing in Lake Martin, and from then on, it should steadily improve."

Despite such restrictions, people fished in the lake's waters and built wooden huts and boats. Old houses in the area were often torn down to acquire lumber to build shelters. Enterprising residents rented boats to fishermen. Fish were thick. J.F. Fargason recalled that the "water in the shallow places was so filled with them one could see and hear them sloshing all around, and some people claimed they could hear them grazing" on inundated crops. Dough balls were a favorite form of fish bait. Fishing and hunting camps appeared along the lake's shoreline near places people considered prime game locations. "Around the rim of Lake Martin are entrancing camp sites," the *Alabama Sportsman* said. "Some persons are already buying acreage for summer homes and camps; several clubs are forming in the state to acquire desirable sites and build camps larger and more pretentious than could be financed by the average individual." The magazine asserted that "no more beautiful scenery can be imagined than that afforded by the rugged hills surrounding this great body of water." *Alabama Sportsman* predicted that the "time is going to come and in

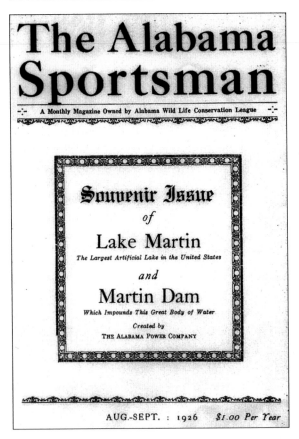

ALABAMA SPORTSMAN *COVER*. *This 1926 edition is the souvenir Lake Martin issue. This magazine included information and stories about the building of Martin Dam and Lake Martin, stocking the lake with fish, and the people who first enjoyed it recreationally.*

no very distant future, when every foot of the acreage abutting on that water is going to be owned by sportsmen and those who want summer homes in the most attractive and ideal location a lover of the out of doors could imagine."

The lake's fluctuating waters sometimes caused problems. In 1926, F.F. Sturdivant and Roy C. Oliver went fishing, but the motor in their boat broke while they were returning to the landing where they had parked their car. "Paddling about among the tree tops of the half flooded basin darkness overtook them and they were unable to locate their car," the *Alabama Sportsman* reported. "Finally reaching land, they built a fire, where they spent the night in intermittent showers of rain." Thinking they had survived calamity, Sturdivant and Oliver were surprised because "When daylight came they discovered themselves on a small island a few hundred yards from the landing." The magazine noted "Neither have suffered any ill-effects from the adventure beyond the discomfort of a sleepless night in the open."

By spring 1927, Lake Martin was almost full. It attracted the attention of *Scientific American*, which featured the lake in the September 1927 issue. In an article entitled, "World's Largest Artificial Lake," the journal reiterated much of the technical information released by the Alabama Power Company. The magazine calculated that "If a person will visualize four straight roads extending from Birmingham to Minneapolis, each having street lights at intervals of 125 feet along each side of the highway, he will obtain a clear conception of the enormous capacity of this new development." The article concluded, "So far as changing the map is concerned, this is one of the most elaborate projects ever undertaken in the southern states."

The dam construction camp was converted into a village for employees working at the dam and their families. Personnel represented various professions, including engineers, electricians, mechanics, carpenters, and apprentices. "It must be remembered that in the late 20s, these people were working on the cutting edge of technology," John Robertson, who lived in the village as a child, commented. "This explains somewhat the remarkable group of people who made their way through the selection process that led to their being residents at the Martin Dam village." He noted that the "demand for their kind of pioneering, like that for their remarkable village, is no more." Many of the dam employees were inventive, innovating technology and designs related to the dam that received patents. The Martin Dam village consisted of approximately 25 green and

INVESTMENT BANKERS. These men visited Martin Dam in early 1927. The New Yorkers recognized the economic potential of the dam and lake.

maroon houses, 2 water tanks, and a store, ice plant, filter plant, clubhouse, bachelor's hall, and pasture. "Runt" O'Daniel ran the village store, and a school was established for the village's children.

The children considered the Martin Dam village and Lake Martin as a Shangri-la, and they were allowed great freedom to roam and explore wherever they wished. The children could play on the dam and were permitted use of boats for adventures on the lake as long as they remained in sight and wore life jackets. If a village child was caught without a life jacket, all of the children were grounded. The children sledded down hills coated with foot-long longleaf pine needles. Robertson remembered, "As Boy Scouts, we 'wilderness camped' in old army pup-tents all around the lake." Whenever Thomas Martin visited Martin Dam, he delighted in the youngsters' antics and insisted on interacting with them.

Beula Golden Ingram, who moved to the village when she was 12, reminisced that the "elevators were one of our favorite places. We would bring kids home from school with us who had never seen an elevator." She humorously recalled, "We would barely open the elevator door so it would stop between floors and scare those kids to death. We were a mischievous bunch." Many of the children had pets, and Ingram played with her cat Nickel. Some children had goats to pull carts. When the Goldens moved, Beula sentimentally stated that "My mama, daddy, and I all cried. It was just one big, happy family at Martin Dam. Those were the happiest, most carefree days of my life."

Erline Dawkins encouraged landscaping of the dam site. The dam's natural rock formation was suitable for a rock garden behind the power plant. Visitors admired the yuccas, caladiums, and other flowers, and the Dawkins family won praise and awards for

GENERATORS AT MARTIN DAM. *These futuristic-looking devices converted Lake Martin's water power into electrical energy.*

their village house yard, which had camellia bushes as high as the eaves and was covered with daffodils. Sometimes storms abruptly hit the lake. "I recall standing near the store, in relatively clear weather," Robertson recalled, "when lightning struck one of the very tall longleaf pines near the lakeshore and you could see the lightning run along the ground stirring up dust as it made its way to the lake." Tornadoes and hurricanes ripped up the lake's timber and shores. Occasionally, snow and ice storms hit, paralyzing the area.

Tourists soon flocked to the new dam and lake. Forty northeastern investment bankers visited Martin Dam in early 1927. Spencer D. Wright of Phil Harrison & Company acknowledged, "Your natural resources are almost unlimited, especially your wealth of water power." Visitor R.J. Gregg was so inspired by the new reservoir that he penned the poem "Lake Martin." The April 1927 *Powergrams* printed Gregg's ode, which depicted the lake as a marvelous place.

> I've stood above Lake Martin
> On a riotous day in spring,
> With all life just surging and singing,
> And my heart was wont to sing.
> And again when all life seemed sleeping,
> And the grass was sere and brown,
> And the heat and hush of noonday,
> Like lead on my soul pressed down.
>
> I've gazed upon Lake Martin
> In the dusk of a Southern day,

CAST MEMBERS OF "THE LAKE." This play was sponsored by the Alabama Power Company, which taught women artificial resuscitation methods for safety at lakes. Pictured here, left to right, are (back row) Miss Howard, Pauline Gibson, Hattie Westmoreland, and Miss Dowd, and (front row) Misses Fuhrman, Ray, and Young.

With the moon and stars a-glisten
On a mirrored Milky Way.

But always, a glance from the mountain,
To the placid lake below,
Filled my soul with wonder,
And set my heart aglow.

For I saw in the quite waters,
'Neath the softly silver sheen,
The strength of countless horses,
Pent up in mountains green.

The heat of Inferno's hottest,
The cold of a winter' snow,
The myriad lights of cities,
The cozy fireside's glow.

I heard the hum of spindles,
The whir and whine of wheels,
The music of many motors,
The click of picture reels.

LABORATORY MODEL. This model was used to test possible flooding scenarios at the dam. Engineers relied on this miniature version of Martin Dam to understand management of water flow.

KOWALIGA CREEK HIGHWAY BRIDGE, 1927. This picture shows the placement of a girder span by floating it into position at the bridge. The bridge girder span was transported by barge to the bridge site.

A panorama wondrous
Of modern hydro-power!
And I thought that there before me,
Gem-set in Beauty's bower.

That the name and deeds of Martin,
Through Time be revered and known.
Was a monument more fitting
Than bronze, or print, or stone.

At the Alabama Power Company's headquarters in Birmingham, the Women's Committee developed a play entitled "The Lake." The power company sponsored this play to teach people artificial resuscitation methods for safety at Alabama's lakes including Lake Martin.

Other people also paid tribute to Lake Martin, but with deeds rather than words. In 1927, Dixie Construction Company completed building the Kowaliga Creek highway bridge. All of the girders and concrete forms were delivered by barge after the lake water reached its maximum height in May 1927. Each girder was 111 feet long and 7.5 feet high. Rigger foreman Robert V. Weaver directed girder placement. *Powergrams* outlined how the work was accomplished:

> By skillfully blocking and skidding, a girder span was placed lengthwise on the
> barge with both ends overhanging. After it was carefully balanced and braced on

HOUSING AT CHEROKEE BLUFFS. *These cabins were built for dam village residents. This isolated community was close-knit and encouraged neighborliness and friendship.*

the barge it was necessary to jack up the span about 10 feet above the floor of the barge so that the ends of the girders would just clear the tops of the piers. The barge was then anchored in exactly the desired position so that when the jacks were released the girders rested in their proper places on the foundations.

Within three weeks, crews had moved all of the girders from the dam to the bridge. *Powergrams* noted that "placing the steel required a high degree of skill and practical experience in rigging, as well as some knowledge of 'seamanship' " and praised Weaver and his associates whose "experience is evident from the fact that the program was carried out expeditiously and without mishap."

Crews surfaced the bridge road and approaches with concrete and rock asphalt. "With only the superstructure and some six or eight feet of the supporting piers showing above the water surface," *Powergrams* commented, "there is little in its appearance today to indicate that a tremendous amount of labor, materials and planning were expended before the structure became a reality." A total of 12,310 truck loads had delivered machines, supplies, food, and lumber to the bridge construction site.

Powergrams credited Lake Martin and Martin Dam with the successful operation of the Upper Tallassee dam when it returned to service in 1928. *Powergrams* declared that the "increased power" of the Upper Tallassee dam "is due in part to the greater height of the dam, but a more important factor is the greater flow of water made possible by the storage in Lake Martin." At the power company's hydraulics laboratory, a model of Martin Dam was used to assess the impact of flowing water on the dam. During the April 1928 flood, 60,000 cubic feet of water poured over the dam every second, and Martin Dam's "stilling basin and banked spillway were given a thorough test at that time."

"A vast lake has buried the ancient town site of Kowaliga," the August 18, 1929, *Montgomery Advertiser* reported. That newspaper printed an interesting article about a surviving Creek cabin from Kowaliga. "When the Alabama Power Company built its great dam across the Tallapoosa River, the water crept back over the land that had once been the site of Kowaliga," reporter William J. Mahoney Jr. noted. "As it moved attention was called to the lone log hut that marked the town's site." Concerned that the hut might be damaged, Peter Brannon, the curator of the Alabama Department of Archives and History, arranged for the structure to be relocated to a fishing camp run by George Todd. Mahoney stated that at that time Tecumseh's Rock "is on an island out in the vast, new lake." Todd transported sightseers in boats to view the rock. Mahoney recalled Kowaliga history, concluding "great schools of fresh water fish now swim by over the site of ancient Kowaliga. Nervous waters of the lake disinter and then rebury relics of the old town. And over it all dangles an occasional baited hook."

Residents purchased land to form camps. Cecil G. Duffee Jr.'s father Cecil and Nell Duffee; Sam and Sara Oliver; Bill and Marion Sheely; Ounce and Clarice Loveland; and Aureyl Young formed the Gay Camp. Mr. Gay of Montgomery sold them the land and a log cabin that he had inherited. The Gay Camp served as a gathering place for fishing and Saturday night meals.

Soon after Lake Martin filled, a group of agriculture engineers at Alabama Polytechnic Institute (modern Auburn University) in nearby Auburn decided that the lake would be a great location for a fishing camp. The agriculture engineers had cooperated with the power company since 1924 in a rural electrification project to develop economical and efficient uses of electricity on Alabama farms, such as dairy refrigeration, water pumping, and grain ginning.

Everett C. Easter, formerly an engineer at the college whom the power company hired in 1927 as their chief agricultural engineer, approached officials with the request from his

DAM VILLAGE SCHOOL AND STUDENTS. Workers' families valued education and made sure it was available for all children.

Auburn colleagues for an outing club. A group of agriculture professors bought land from B.W. Gates that bordered the lake at Blue Creek to form an Auburn colony. The power company had purchased contiguous land from Gates that was under the high-water mark. The agricultural engineers wanted to affirm their right to use the land along the shore and receive permission to initiate improvements on the beach. The Auburn engineers and agriculturists were among the first people to develop the lake for leisure activities.

The power company granted permission to the engineers and agricultural faculty to build their camp on the lake's shore. The camp's deed was halved, with Mark Nichols and agricultural engineers J.B. Wilson, Arvy Carnes, and John W. Randolph buying one-half of the land, and Dean Funchess, F.W. Parker, W.D. Salmon, and R.Y. Bailey and members of the agricultural school's staff purchasing the remaining title. The power company, eager to cooperate, signed a lease with the group, requiring that they pay $1 to be granted the privilege of using the lake for recreation.

The Auburn professors built a cabin, boathouse, and cook shack. They brought their children to the lake while they constructed the buildings and often worked until dark. They brought blankets and pillows to sleep on the ground. The children teased local superintendent of schools "Judge" Parish about his fear of reptiles, warning him that there were plenty of snakes waiting to crawl over them while they slept. During the night the boys rigged up a facsimile of a snake to wake Parish up as it was maneuvered inside his blankets. When he felt the fake snake against his skin, he mistook it as the real thing— leaping out of his blankets and running into the woods—much to the young lads' delight.

Weekly visits to Lake Martin promised exciting adventures to the colony families who swam and played games. They had fish fries, barbecues, and picnics. After dinner, dances were held, and the camp inhabitants enjoyed singing and playing musical instruments under the starry sky.

BOYS ON PONIES. *Shown here at the Cherokee Bluffs dam village, these two identified boys and ponies enjoy an afternoon of exploring the piney woods.*

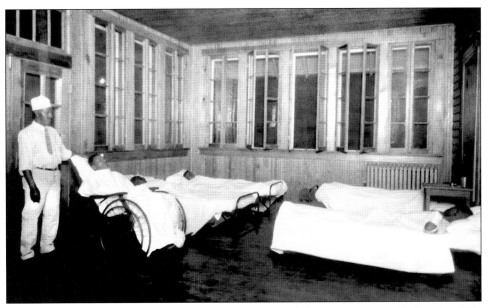

HOSPITAL WARD AT THE DAM. *These unidentified patients enjoy fresh air while convalescing.*

Auburn's student agricultural engineering club initiated new members at the camp by blindfolding them in the woods and instructing them to find the cabin. Most students fumbled and stumbled through the woods, tripping over roots and sticks and running into trees. Nichols was particularly impressed by the cleverness of one initiate who gathered a handful of rocks and pebbles after he was masked; the student threw the stones to determine what obstacles surrounded him, following the pings as rocks fell into the lake or hit the ground or trees, until he located the path to the cabin, successfully returning to the group unscathed.

The Auburn agricultural engineers valued their camp at Lake Martin so much that they mentioned it in advertising and correspondence to recruit new professors. The research conducted in the department was conducive to their recreational pursuits at Lake Martin and its nearby communities. The engineers cooperated with the fisheries department to study pond hydraulics and create better habitats for fish. They surveyed buildings to improve the quality of houses and farm structures and analyzed soils in Tallapoosa County. The engineers worked closely with Tallapoosa County agents Samuel M. Day and Fletcher N. Farrington, in cooperation with county bankers, judges, and commissioners, such as John Elkins, to conserve soil, improve land values, and increase farmer's profits.

With assistance from Auburn's agricultural engineers, Tallapoosa County terracing clubs and cooperative associations were able to help farmers share expensive equipment at low costs. The engineers demonstrated how to use tractors and cultivators to save labor, increase yields, and cultivate profits. They also studied better methods of fire protection, land clearing through drainage and blasting (showing farmers how to distill turpentine from removed stumps for extra monetary gain), and syrup manufacturing.

MARTIN DAM DEDICATION CEREMONY. From left to right are Dr. J.M. Starke, Thomas W. Martin, Colonel Oliver R. Hood, and Benjamin Russell.

The Auburn Lake Martin colony was sold for taxes in the summer of 1943. At that time, most of Auburn's faculty were serving in World War II and unaware that such obligations had not been paid. Auburn engineer J.B. Wilson went to Dadeville in December 1943 to reclaim the property by paying $12 in back taxes. According to sources, Wilson was the last known owner of the property, and records do not indicate if Auburn's agricultural community returned to the camp after the war.

Most probably, the campsite was abandoned as various individuals bought acreage and built more elaborate fishing cabins and weekend homes. The Auburn agricultural engineering camp, a representative of Lake Martin's earliest history, symbolized the enjoyment and relaxation that the lake has offered to many generations since its creation.

President Franklin D. Roosevelt visited Elmore County in the 1930s and might have seen the new Martin dam and lake. During the Depression, Works Projects Administration writers prepared a WPA guide to Alabama. The writers described the 1930s Lake Martin, saying "its arms reach back along the river's former watercourses into rugged, heavily timbered hills." The passage told readers that "In spring, azalea, honeysuckle, and dogwood border the cool, shady waters that eventually narrow down to trickling brooks." Sportsmen could test their skills at the lake, which "contains calico, large-mouthed, and small-mouthed bass, and speedy robins, or rose-breasted bream. In addition to game fish there are many bottom-feeding species." Around the lake, "In season, hunting for rabbits, squirrels, quail and turkey is good." The guide also noted that the Alabama Power Company owned most of the land adjacent to the lake and that "camping is permitted with the request that caution be taken to prevent forest fires." The power company established a pine tree seed bed nursery in 1934, and workers began planting seedlings the next year. Alabama Power also gave land for a tower for forest fire control. In 1935, Lake Mead, the reservoir of Hoover Dam, surpassed Lake Martin as the world's largest artificial lake.

Although Thomas Martin humbly did not want a formal naming ceremony dedicating Martin Dam, the Alabama Power Company's board of directors convinced him that such a celebration was appropriate. Martin "consented to the ceremony but only on the condition that the occasion would be an informal meeting of those identified with the work of the Company over many years." He also wanted to include citizens from Elmore and Tallapoosa Counties.

On September 17, 1936, the power company's board of directors passed a resolution to dedicate the dam that had been named a decade prior by a 1926 resolution. The purpose of this ceremony was that a "suitable plate or tablet be placed and unveild [sic]" and to give "proper recognition to the work and labors of Mr. Martin in hydro-electric development in the Southeast and for the progress and upbuilding of his native State." The board noted that Martin Dam deserved a formal dedication because, since 1926, "this great project . . . has added its power to the resources of the Company and to the progress and development of the State."

Benjamin Russell served as chairman of the October 16, 1936, dedication ceremonies at Martin Dam, and he told the crowd that "November 7, 1925, at this site on the Tallapoosa River, was a memorable day. A day of far-reaching promise for Alabama. On that day the corner stone was laid for a development to give nature a chance to ease the burdens of humanity." He reminded listeners that "This development at that time was

THOMAS W. MARTIN. Martin is shown here at the Cherokee Bluffs dam during the 1936 Martin Dam and Lake Martin dedication.

spoken of as the thirteen million dollar Cherokee Bluffs power project and as the Cherokee Bluffs Dam of the Alabama Power Company." Russell announced that "we meet here today to dedicate Martin Dam to the service of the living generation and to generations yet unborn."

Letters from two Alabama Power Company pioneers were read at the ceremony. Captain W.P. Lay wrote Martin that the "Dam had borne your name so long that I had lost sight of the fact that it had not been formally dedicated." Company senior vice-president Colonel Reuben A. Mitchell praised Martin for his "upbuilding of Alabama and the South and the advancement of the electric industry." Colonel Oliver R. Hood spoke of the Alabama Power Company's origins and how Martin Dam had helped the company grow. He nostalgically narrated how the "beautiful river, the Tallapoosa, brings to us wondrously interesting stories of fact and romance" and how Martin Dam and Lake had been created in a "primeval and almost limitless forests."

Russell spoke again, continuing the laudatory commentary about Martin:

> As I look upon this magnificent Martin Dam, its body poured of concrete, standing fearless to the elements, I remember that he who was at the helm in its building has vision, was talented, was courageous, was endowed with an intellectual power bent upon creating electric power.
>
> I gaze upon that beautiful, quiet, deep and powerful body of water known as Lake Martin. Its surface all serene except for the lap of its waves on the shores; and I know that for whom this great lake is named, is

MARTIN DAM MONUMENT. Thomas Martin Tyson and Martin Westgate McWhorter unveiled the monument.

MALARIAL CONTROL SPRAY BOATS. Workers, armed with deadly insecticide, float near Lake Martin's shoreline where mosquitoes lay their eggs.

esteemed for his unstained character. For his modesty. For his great depth of conviction and determination to battle fearlessly for the preservation of that which is the right, and for the betterment of humankind.

The characteristic of Martin Dam and Martin Lake are symbolized in the person of Thomas Wesley Martin, who as president of the Alabama Power Company brought them into being.

Martin responded with a lengthy speech and by expressing the "sense of obligation I feel to the thousands of men and women, including the pioneers, who have made this development possible." He thanked lake area residents for their "personal sacrifice" that enabled the dam and lake to be created. "It is my wish that this structure which you unveil today should stand as emblematic of those pioneer spirits to whom I have referred," he said, "as well as the members of the organization—the living as well as the dead." He emphasized that the power company had created safety methods for Martin Dam, but that some fatal accidents had occurred during construction. "I wish to pause and pay a special tribute to the following men who gave their lives in the construction of the plant," Martin solemnly stated before reciting the list of casualties: "James Huston, W.F. Hamilton, Vincent Henderson, Joe Fleming, Robert Johnston, L.B. Patterson, J.F. Foreman, Millard Simpson, and T.J. Campbell."

Two young boys, Thomas Martin Tyson and Martin Westgate McWhorter, both named for Martin, had been chosen to pull the cord unveiling the marker. Hugh Martin had designed the huge monument, which John Thornberg had sculpted.

Technical improvements at the dam included a relay system, put in place by 1940, that established transmission lines to nearby communities and as far as Leeds and Anniston, Alabama, and to Georgia. J.W. Graff and J.N. Stewart monitored the Martin Dam relay system that maintained power service during lightning storms, inclement weather, or

"TALLASSEE ON THE MARCH" PARADE. This Alabama Power Company float was built by Martin Dam employees on December 10, 1940. Pictured here, left to right, are Kathleen Wade, Rachel Daniel, and Joyce Hawkins.

other mechanical disruptions. Faulty lines were temporarily disconnected so that other lines could function. In 1941, telemetering enabled remote monitoring of transmission line load flow so that Martin Dam's generators could be adjusted accordingly. Speed control devices meant that the dam's turbine gates could be fully open from a closed position in 20 seconds. Previously, that action had taken 100 seconds.

In 1940, a crew of Martin Dam employees deployed seven malarial control spray boats they had built. The motorized vessels were equipped with pumps that discharged 300 gallons of spray daily, but workers also used hand sprayers to apply a mixture of 80 percent kerosene and 20 percent black oil combined with water. Two to five people manned each boat, moving along the shoreline where mosquitoes gathered to lay eggs in the shallow water. One person navigated the boat, while another crew member aimed the nozzle "here and there wherever there may be a likelihood for the establishment of aviation schools for flying musketeers." Knapsack boats were designed to move through the shallowest water, particularly in grassy and willow-lined inlets, where other boats could not easily pass. The mosquito boats were outfitted with screens over the pump intakes to prevent sand from clogging the pumps, and steel cages protected propellers from underwater stumps. Air tanks were placed for temporary buoyancy to slow sinking in case the boats were damaged by storms or leaks. Sometimes crews playfully sprayed passing cars when their boats were going underneath the Kowaliga Bridge. The Lake Martin malaria control methods were adopted internationally.

The December 1940 "Martin Dam Notes" revealed details about the lake's surrounding community. The Martin Dam Camp had hosted its annual barbecue on November 11 for residents and visitors. Announcements told that "Born to Mr. and Mrs. W.F. Murphy, November 3, a daughter, Dorthy Claudia. Mrs. Murphy is daughter of Mr. and Mrs. J.W. Peeples of Martin Dam" and "Bobby Dawkins spent Thanksgiving with his parents, Mr. and Mrs. R.D. Dawkins." Dawkins's sister Emagene (Jean) Dawkins Davidson had also visited her family at the dam. Notices of dam village residents buying land and building homes in nearby communities was also included.

The news also provided technical information such as the fact that 23-million kilowatt hours had been generated in November. Readers were told that "Plastering and painting of the switch board room and superintendent's office and painting of the metal sash windows in power house has been completed. Erection of fences and flood lights will be completed soon."

Martin Dam was represented at the "Tallassee on the March" parade and historical pageant on December 10, 1940. The parade celebrated the dedication of Benjamin Fitzpatrick bridge adjacent to Thurlow Dam on the Tallapoosa River. The Alabama Power Company float paid tribute to the three power generating plants the company had built in the Tallapoosa River basin. J.R. House, a power company assistant advertising manager, designed the float, and Martin Dam employees R.H. Copeland and C.F. Pierce built it with him. Joyce Harkins, daughter of Mr. and Mrs. Clyde Harkins of the Martin Dam village, rode on the float, holding a Martin Dam shield.

A 1941 drought dried up a large portion of Lake Martin. By late November 1940, the lake had already dropped 22 feet, and an observer commented that "Over half of the water is gone." By New Year's Day 1941, Martin Dam had operated continuously for 14 years with no time lost due to accidents. Over 2.5-million man hours had been invested in dam

LAKE MARTIN DROUGHT, 1941. This view of a bridge shows how drastically the lake level dropped.

operation and maintenance, including malarial spraying, and 5-billion kilowatt hours generated during that time. Martin Dam personnel and their families celebrated at a February 17 chicken barbecue held in the village clubhouse. *Powergrams* printed news J.B. Shannon supplied, including "Born, Jan. 24 to Mr. and Mrs. L.A. Achimon, a son whom they have named Richard Stanley" and "Mrs. P. Loomis is back at home, recovering from an operation at the Tallassee hospital."

World War II affected Martin Dam. Because they were isolated, residents who did not listen to their radios did not immediately learn about the attack on Pearl Harbor. Beula Golden Ingram remembered that one "morning my daddy [Carson Golden] looked out the window and there was a soldier marching up and down by our back door. We didn't know what had happened." She recalled, "My daddy asked the soldier what he was doing. He said that Pearl Harbor had been attacked the night before." The soldiers had been assigned from Fort McClellan to guard Martin Dam throughout World War II. "They had fig newtons, which we did not have," Robertson remembered. "They shared them despite our having thrown firecrackers at their feet!" The soldiers lived in what were called the "Bachelors Quarters," which was the hospital that had been built for dam construction.

Personnel tightened security to reduce the risk of sabotage. Ingram explained that "My daddy had to show a pass to go from the dam to anywhere else in the camp. We all had to have a pass to get out and go anywhere." Robertson recalled that during the war "there was a chain link fence gate at the end of the dam. It had barbed wire across the top and long metal spikes extending out over each side (one over the lake and the other off the 100-something foot drop off the lower side of the dam)." He humorously commented, "It may have been effective against intruders but it scarcely slowed down the village kids who considered it something of an obstacle course!"

MULTI-PURPOSE BARGE. This boat was used as a filling station, power plant, and mosquito control craft on early Lake Martin.

During the war, Navy patrol pilots landed on the lake near the village because they had engine trouble but probably most likely because they enjoyed eating meals prepared by Jasper Moon at the village's guest house. The mosquito boats retrieved the crews and brought them to the village. After replacement engines arrived, workers used big cranes on the dam to lower the engines into place on the airplanes.

Village residents patriotically supported the war effort. Vernon A. Baker, chairman of the dam's safety committee, reported in the April 1943 *Powergrams* that the dam had completed 16 years "without a lost time accident" and "Of this record we are truly proud, as we should be." Baker jokingly said, "We have our fingers crossed, and upon the person of any Martin Dam employee one might, on close examination, find any number of good luck charms—rabbit feet, horse shoes, etc." He remarked that "we're not unduly superstitious, but are more than anxious to keep our much treasured record unbroken. At present we are working, eating and sleeping SAFELY—we hope." He also elaborated about how the war was altering the dam's workforce. "We now have one problem to deal with; that is the stream of new men coming into our ranks from over the system." He welcomed the men because "they're good-natured and safety-minded" and "along with the valuable instructions that they have already received, we feel that again we can make the grade. And when December 31, 1943 comes 'round we hope to have attained another rung on our Safety Ladder of Success."

At the safety celebratory barbecue prepared by Duke Woodson, "Each person was served an ample plate (not so much as on past occasions of this kind, in keeping with the times) of barbecued chicken, potato salad and pickle. Soft drinks were served as desired by the individual." The audience was filled with "so large a number of greasy faces" as people watched the movie *I Am An American* presented by General Motors. Alabama Power Company representatives R.L. Harris and J.O. Henkel Jr. discussed safety goals before the director of safety J.O. Speed presented a plaque to Superintendent Dawkins. Presents and prizes were distributed, including seed for the dam's victory garden.

Two World War II military aircraft crashed at Lake Martin. African-American pilots from Moton Field at the Tuskegee Institute flew over Lake Martin during training missions, and the Tuskegee Airmen's drills included learning low-altitude acrobatic maneuvers. Some Tuskegee Airmen in the 99th Pursuit Squadron became bored because they were not sent to theatres of war in Europe and North Africa after they received their silver wings and qualified for combat missions. Disappointed by being kept in Alabama and away from action, these pilots often engaged in risky maneuvers to test their piloting skills.

Prior to being sent overseas in April 1943, the Tuskegee Airmen dared each other to fly underneath the Kowaliga Bridge. Chief C. Alfred Anderson, who directed pilot training, remembered that "frustrated black pilots did all kinds of ridiculous things to let off steam" and that "six or seven killed themselves in unnecessary accidents." The first death occurred during a June 8, 1942, training mission. Two Tuskegee Airmen, Cadets Richard "Red" Dawson and Walter I. Lawson, did not clear the lake water when they flew their AT-6 beneath Kowaliga Bridge. The propeller hit the water, flipping the plane and breaking it in two. Dawson died on impact. Charles W. Dryden remembered that "Cadet Walter I. Lawson was found sitting on the bank of the river, dazed and bruised, but alive.

ROCK GARDEN. *The Alabama Power Company landscaped Martin Dam with this rock garden.*

Miraculously, surprisingly alive! Not surprisingly he became nicknamed 'Ghost' Lawson." Residents saw the damaged airplane being carried away on a truck. Later, Lawson was among the first Tuskegee Airmen sent to Europe, where he excelled as a combat pilot.

In March 1945, a B-25 bomber crashed into Lake Martin during a thunderstorm, and its mysterious disappearance into the lake's depths was the topic of early lake lore. The front page of the March 22, 1945, *Montgomery Advertiser* proclaimed, "Army Bomber Missing on Flight to City." On March 20, the plane was flying between Washington, D.C., and Fort Worth, Texas, on a combat training mission. Military personnel at Bolling Field said that radio contact with the twin-engine bomber ended after pilot Army Captain John Glenn Mabry established contact at 10:13 in the morning in Atlanta. He never radioed to operators at Montgomery, which was his next scheduled refueling stop. Twenty-five planes flew from Gunter Field along a 50-mile corridor of Mabry's flight path on March 23, but were unable to find the overdue bomber. In addition to Mabry from east St. Louis, Illinois, two crew members, Captain Charles P. Oliver of Penacook, New Hampshire, and aerial engineer Staff Sergeant James N. Green from Washington, were missing. Rumors circulated that the airplane had sunk in Lake Martin, but the facts remained elusive for several decades.

Because people reported hearing an explosion and seeing an oil slick and debris on the lake near Sandy Creek, the military deployed a naval diving crew from Pensacola soon after the plane disappeared. The Navy divers removed the bomber's engines, leaving them in the lake because they were too heavy and deep in muddy water for easy retrieval. When the Air Force tried to pull the plane out with a cable, the tail section broke, and Green's body was retrieved. Misidentifying the body as Oliver, the military informed his widow, Virginia Oliver, who planned a funeral. His hometown newspaper told that "Capt. Oliver was on a test flight from Washington to Texas at the time his plane crashed. His body was found in Lake Martin, Ala., on Easter Sunday." Further military salvage efforts ceased. In the 1990s, Bob Norwood located and began to salvage the bomber.

Lake Martin became a popular vacation spot after World War II, as people celebrated the war's end by spending more leisure time with their families. The booming post–World War II economy meant that many people had enough money to indulge in cars to drive to the lake. Some even purchased boats; houseboats, pontoons, paddleboats, and aluminum crafts became popular. Local businesses benefited by offering lodging, meals, and fishing gear and supplies to Lake Martin customers. "It was a big surprise to many of us when we returned home from our various military services to see a beautiful blue water lake," Cecil G. Duffee Jr. said. "They say all the young men left and the older men stopped farming which allowed the land to grow up in trees and the trees stopped the erosion of the red clay that is typical of the piedmont section." Duffee exclaimed, "For whatever reason Lake Martin was a jewel!"

Recreational fishing and boating flourished at Lake Martin. The state game department stocked Lake Martin with several types of fish, and the Alabama Water Improvement Commission stated that the lake's water was safe for contact sports. Many people used cane poles to fish from piers where large fish were rumored to dwell. Others cast tempting lures into the lake's clear, deep waters accessible only by boat. People enjoyed Fourth of July fish fries with tables full of coleslaw and hush puppies, and holiday parades of decorated boats. Teenagers flirted on the lake's beaches. Sportsmen competed in fishing and water skiing contests and boat races. Area scout troops regularly camped at Lake Martin, testing their skills with rods and reels and watercraft.

MARTIN DAM LIBRARY. The library was established by Erline Dawkins and Margaret Fell Johnson.

MARTIN DAM LIBRARY. These girls are enjoying reading magazines. The Martin Dam Library subscribed to popular periodicals, which met the varying interests of patrons.

The Alabama Power Company realized that Alabamians sought more leisure activities. The company began a recreation program in 1948 with a supervisor at Lake Martin who urged public use of the lake. Alabama Power sponsored annual fishing contests during the next decade. The "Whopper Catcher Contest" offered prizes, including money, certificates, and trophies for various fish species and sizes caught. This program continued for several years. Anglers could take fish to stores where official weigh-in officers weighed the fish and notified the Alabama Power Company. Participants then received a certificate and letter like the one Jess "Ruth" Hall and Berta Pogue got after weighing a fish at W.T. Farrow's Blue Creek store. J.G. Hitchcock, the power company's land department manager, wrote the following:

> This is to certify that Mrs. Jess Hall and Mrs. Berta Pogue did on May 6, 1952, catch from Martin Lake, during the period of Alabama Power Company's fishing contest, a large-mouthed bass weighing 6 lbs. and 9 ozs. And by reason thereof is a member of the "Whopper-Catchers Club."

The Russell Corporation moved 600 houses from its textile mill village to the lake in 1946 and rented them to employees for less than $10 per month and also to vacationers. These green cabins were a common sight at the early lake. Mill executives built more elaborate cabins for weekend use and hosted state and national leaders, who invested in lake property. Jean Henderson remembered that "Russell had a place on the lake called Piney Woods, which was a place they let employees' children go in the summer, but really anyone in Alexander City could go to the lake and stay for days." The Russell family also opened Wind Creek Park in the 1950s. That site later was designated a state park and renovated through the 1980s, becoming Alabama's largest camping park.

Lake Martin was also home to a unique library. At the annual Martin Dam barbecue on May 24, 1946, Thomas Martin remarked that a dam library would enhance the rural community. Residents suggested that the library could serve as a memorial to World War II soldiers from the community, including the Dawkins's son Bobby, who had died in the Philippines when his B-24 bomber was shot down. A suitable building in the village was prepared, and Martin and his wife, power company employees, and dam villagers donated books. Alabama Power Company librarian Margaret Fell Johnson traveled from Birmingham to assist in the cataloging of more than 1,000 books, including both fiction and non-fiction. The library had almanacs, city directories, magazines, and a museum section with a button-up shoe collection. Johnson commented, "Because of its remoteness, this collection of books is of unusual value, and I can think of no more perfect sanctuary than a quiet corner in one of these well-lighted rooms with a favorite book."

During the Thomas Wesley Martin Library dedication on May 21, 1949, Reverend Mr. Selman Bradley, minister at the Tallassee Methodist Church, led the crowd in prayer. "We thank Thee for the institution of this library in this community," he said, "which will serve as a place for the harnessing of natural resources of the human mind and spirit, and enable the people who use the facilities here to make their lives instruments of service to their fellowmen."

Martin commented about the dam village residents: "Here they have made their home and their friends and here their family has grown up. It seemed to them very fitting that the community should have a library." He credited Erline Dawkins enthusiastic work as

TALLASSEE YOUTH CAMP. Area children gathered for the dedication of the camp at Lake Martin on May 29, 1949.

dam librarian as the reason for the library's success. Martin praised Superintendent Dawkins, saying "I want to pay my tribute to you, Mrs. Dawkins, and those associated with you, for the magnificent job you have done in operating this plant." Commenting on the stressful World War II years, Martin thanked the dam employees, acknowledging that the "strain under which you and all of us have worked the past few years, the difficult problems we have had, the manner in which you have kept this plant going to meet ever-increasing demands for power—have been an inspiration to us all." He reminded the crowd of the importance of their work, promising

> a new Alabama and a new South, soon to come into its own rightful place: a South that would retain all the finest traditions of its glorious past, but which, through that mysterious force flowing silently through the thousands of miles of transmission lines, like life-blood to the human body, would grow richer and stronger industrially, and because of this would in turn grow stronger agriculturally. And the chain lengthens. Not only would the ordinary creature comforts follow in the wake of electricity, but there would be better educational facilities, better roads, and better homes. To make money is all right. To build any industry is fine. To build an industry that saves mankind from toil that it can well be spared, that reduces the labor and drudgery of women and so provides leisure for education and culture, truly is a much finer thing.

Speakers included 14-year-old John Ashley Robertson, Erline Dawkins's nephew, who had lived in the village. As an adult, Robertson recalled how he worked diligently on his speech, selecting words exactly to express a lot in the short period of time he was allotted to speak.

One week later, the Tallassee Youth Camp was dedicated at Lake Martin on May 29, 1949. The camp was established for community use, but especially for scout and church youth groups. Reverend Selman Bradley, who was the catalyst for the camp's establishment, stated that camp access was available to "any organization whose purpose is building Christian character among young people." The camp consisted of concrete block buildings for housing, dining, and meetings. More than 100 people attended the dedication ceremony where Martin urged schools to offer additional instruction in Alabama and United States history to insure "leaders of tomorrow, the children present here today, might know more of the men and women who have made their state and nation great."

6. Vacationers and Developers: 1950s through the 1970s

From the 1950s through the 1970s, development of Lake Martin property significantly expanded and enhanced the lake's natural resources. As more people learned about Lake Martin, additional recreational and housing facilities became necessary. The Alabama Power Company leased affordable sites for cottages. More people from communities near the lake or southern urban areas built small lakeside cabins for weekend retreats. Lake Martin's shores sported various structures and resorts. Zipp Newman, a *Birmingham News* sports editor, declared that Lake Martin was "positively one of the most fabulous playgrounds in America." By the late 1960s, an estimated 2 million people enjoyed Lake Martin annually.

The Martin Dam visitors reception building was opened in 1950 and the road from Walnut Hill to Martin Dam was paved. Martin Dam promoted interaction with the engineering departments at the nearby Alabama Polytechnic Institute, and many Alabama Power Company employees were Auburn alumni. On May 6, 1950, students of Professors James Chadwick and Albert Sprague visited Martin Dam. Dam superintendent Dawkins, assistant superintendent Couch, and southern division manager B.B. Marsh encouraged the students to explore the dam and consider hydroelectric careers.

Auburn's fisheries department aided in the improvement of Lake Martin. Because the "imbalance of fish and available food produced slim prospects for a creel limit," Dr. Homer S. Swingle from Auburn cooperated with personnel from the Alabama Conservation Department to seek a solution. They "decided to introduce threadfin shad from the Coosa to Lake Martin as a source of fish food. Immediately good fishing resulted."

A May 19, 1950 barbecue at Martin Dam celebrated the fifth consecutive year of dam operation without any accidents occurring, and Alabama Power Company representatives presented a safety certificate to dam superintendent Dawkins. Games with prizes were featured for children at the picnic. "The unplanned event, but joyously received nevertheless, was a downpour," *Powergrams* reported, explaining "while it mired up some of the cars, cut down on the attendance and softened some straw hats and uncreased clothes and made driving hazardous," the storm "made brooks into creeks and creeks into rivers, giving Martin Dam almost that extra two feet needed to fill it."

KOWALIGA MARINA. This boat is being carried from storage to the lake. Returning boats to the water from land-based warehouses is a frequent sight as vacationers return to Lake Martin.

The Alabama Power Company supported civic improvement of the Tallapoosa River area. In spring 1950, the company provided funds to build a school at Zana on the river's east side because many African-American students living there had no way to cross to the school on the west side of the river. The power company also promoted reforestation, agricultural diversification, and soil conservation in an effort to stop top soil from washing into the river and lake.

The Cold War intensified security around Lake Martin, and the Martin Dam Civil Defense Area committee was organized to "protect against subversive or enemy action." According to the September 5, 1950 *Alexander City Outlook*, Colonel Ira Thompson, state civilian defense director, "warned of present and future peril unless citizens stay on their toes here and keep on the lookout for Communists and saboteurs in the Martin Dam area."

Although vigilant, residents and visitors also played at the lake. In the 1950s, two marinas, Kowaliga and Real Island Marina, were built at Lake Martin to cater to the growing lake population. At Tom Russell's request, John "Toppy" and Charlotte Hodnett opened the Kowaliga Restaurant, grocery, and cabins in 1952. Kowaliga was the site of Lake Martin's first sizable community. As many as 10,000 people visited on weekend afternoons. The Kowaliga Inn offered rental cottages and fishing and pleasure boats to vacationers. Paddleboats rented at the rate of $1 per day, and people enjoyed walking, lounging, and playing on the man-made sand beaches. Russell opened a sports shop, and a World War II fighter pilot ran a repair service. Governor Jim Folsom passed through

Elmore County when he was running for election, and he may have visited the emerging Lake Martin community to campaign.

National champion water skier Leah Rawls Atkins and her husband George, an Auburn football player, lived at Kowaliga after they married in 1954. Leah taught water skiing, and George worked as a lifeguard and waiter to supplement his football scholarship to pay their college tuition. The couple participated in some notable Lake Martin firsts. Toppy Hodnett asked them to help set up a jump and slalom course at Kowaliga, and Leah Rawls Atkins performed Sunday water ski shows. She also had an interesting encounter on Lake Martin. Seeing a stalled boater waving a white towel, Atkins rescued Governor Gordon Persons who needed to be towed to his Lake Martin home.

At times, the lake was dangerous. Bill Teague recalled that during the 1950s, some submerged tree ties "began breaking loose and suddenly a log, some as long as seventy feet, would shoot up out of the water twenty feet into the air like a cannon ball." Teague explained that because these trees were "water-logged," they would "float unseen right beneath the surface, waiting to tear up a boat or a prop."

Lake Martin inspired country music legend Hank Williams Sr. to write the hit song "Kaw-Liga." Area residents Darwin Dobbs, WRFS disc jockey Bob McKinnon, and radio station manager Charles Whatley visited with Hank Williams in Nashville, Tennessee. Dobbs invited Williams to stay at Dobbs's Lake Martin cabin whenever he needed a retreat. Darwin and his wife Nell had built the cabin in 1946. Williams, a Montgomery native, was interested in the lake area and had conducted interviews with McKinnon for

SAILBOATING, 1950s. Sailboats became popular at Lake Martin in this decade. These elegant watercraft create picturesque scenes on the lake.

DARWIN DOBBS'S CABIN. Hank Williams Sr. wrote "Kaw-Liga" here. From the porch, visitors can see a broad expanse of Lake Martin.

his radio show. While he stayed at Lake Martin in August 1952 to recuperate after he was fired from the Grand Ole Opry, Williams wrote two classic songs, "Kaw-Liga" and "Your Cheatin' Heart." He also performed at the Red Hill School auditorium.

During his Lake Martin sojourn, Williams was jailed for disorderly conduct. He had been wading in the lake when a group of fans saw him and gave him a jug of corn liquor, and he became drunk. Alexander City police chief Winfred Patterson arrested Williams at the Alexander City Hotel on August 17, 1952. The *Alabama Journal* later reported Patterson described Williams "more or less was having DTs (delirium tremens). He was running up and down the hall, yelling that somebody was whipping old ladies and he was going to stop them."

The next day, Williams bought tires at Dobbs's automobile dealership to reimburse him for use of the cabin. That night, Williams wrote the lyrics for "Kaw-Liga" with a tablet and pencil in the Dobbs's cabin. There are several versions of how Williams wrote the song. The account many people support claim that Williams was inspired late one evening while riding in a Cadillac to buy alcohol from a bootlegger in Kellyton. He had been at a party at Kowaliga with McKinnon and other Lake Martin friends when they decided to buy more to drink.

"I feel a song coming on," Williams reportedly said in the car, "I just have the strangest feeling about it." Talking about Lake Martin, Williams remarked, "It's such a beautiful place. And I think about the Indians and I think about the water and how beautiful it is." He began tapping rhythmically on the dashboard and saying the name "Kowaliga." Williams became restless and urged, "Bob, hurry back. Let's get back on down to the lake.

I've got it now. I know what I want now." Williams also wrote "Your Cheatin' Heart" and "Lonesomest Time of the Day" at Kowaliga before going to Montgomery. He asked Fred Rose to travel to Alabama to compose music. Rose retitled Williams's "Kowaliga" as "Kaw-Liga" and focused the story to feature a dime-store Indian.

The lyrics of "Kaw-Liga" are based on a love story that was often told around the lake about a Creek chief, Kowaliga, who lived in the area where Kowaliga marina and restaurant were later built. Kowaliga loved a maiden whose father had already arranged her marriage. After his beloved departed, the despairing Kowaliga became rooted by the shore, hoping she would return. He waited so long in one place that he became wooden and rooted to the spot.

> Kawliga was a wooden Indian standing by the door
> He fell in love with an Indian maiden over in the antique store
> Kaw Li Ga
>
> Just stood there and never let it show
> So she could never answer yes or no

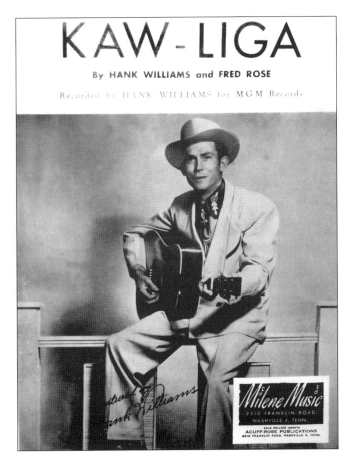

"KAW-LIGA" SHEET MUSIC. Country music fans can play and sing this number-one hit themselves.

He always wore his Sunday feathers and held a tomahawk
The maiden wore her beads and braids and hoped some day he'd talk
Kaw Li Ga
Too stubborn to ever show a sign
Because his heart was made of knotty pine

Poor ol' Kaw Li Ga, he never got a kiss
Poor ol' Kaw Li Ga, he don't know what he missed
Is it any wonder that his face is red
Kaw Li Ga, that poor ol' wooden head
Kawliga was a wooden Indian, never went nowhere
His Heart was set on the Indian maiden with the coal black hair
Kaw Li Ga
Just stood there and never let it show
So she could never answer yes or no
And then one day a wealthy customer bought the Indian maid
And took her oh so far away but ol Kaw Li Ga stayed
Kaw Li Ga

Just stands there as lonely as can be
And wishes he was still an old pine tree

INTERIOR OF DOBBS'S CABIN. In 2002, the furnishings of this famous Lake Martin cabin were reproduced based on photographs taken at the time Hank Williams Sr. stayed there.

CHURCH IN THE PINES. *Generations of Lake Martin residents have worshiped here both in the arbor and in boats floating nearby.*

Williams performed "Kaw-Liga" during his final recording session on September 23, 1952 in Nashville. In 1953, "Kaw-Liga" became a number one hit country song and the best-selling country record for that year after Williams's unexpected death of a heart attack on the previous New Year's Day.

Williams never saw the plaster Kowaliga that stood guard at Cecil's on the Lake restaurant for several decades. After Williams's visit, McKinnon and Colonel Sim Wilbanks went to Sylacauga's Castleberry Motor Company and asked the dealership for the Pontiac Motors Indian used to promote cars. Jim Whatley joined the pair to convince Williams's widow "Miss Audrey" to perform at the restaurant. They gave the Indian to the restaurant. Souvenir hunters took pieces of the original Kowaliga, which was replaced.

The Church in the Pines was built on Russell Mills property by the Kowaliga Bridge so that Lake Martin residents and visitors had a special place to worship. Julia Walker Russell, wife of Thomas D. Russell, led the effort to establish the Church in the Pines. The church and its wooden cross and rock pulpit became a prominent Lake Martin landmark. In his history of the church, Ben Russell recalled, "Our little Church in the Pines began in 1953 under a small, pine-straw covered arbor on the 750 miles of shoreline of a yet undiscovered (5-10 year-round inhabitants) and rather new Lake Martin." Russell said, "Over time, the little congregation grew and grew, dovetailing nicely into the mores of this closely knit lake community of the early fifties." The church enabled people to stay all weekend at the lake without shirking religious observations.

Services were nondenominational, and ministers from local churches rotated Sunday services. Russell explained that ministers "coveted an invitation, as they were well fed and entertained at the lake 'cabin' of a proud member of their flock." Ministers were presented brown sacks with the congregation's offering for the ministers' churches. Sermons often

CHURCH IN THE PINES PULPIT. *The stone, book-shaped pulpit has witnessed many Lake Martin services and celebrations, including weddings and christenings.*

included passages from noted novels, specifically *To Kill a Mockingbird* written by Alabamian Harper Lee.

Russell told how "many of the congregation arrived in a rather motley collection of watercraft." Children especially enjoyed going to church in a boat. Russell described the waterfront congregation as "being to the utter astonishment and sheer delight of the younger set, many managing to remain aboard or, in the case of the more incorrigibles, thereabouts." He humorously noted the noise associated with church services, saying "Experience generally prevailed, however, with the lot, dogs and all, being anchored a distance off shore."

Worshippers anxiously awaited the weekly address, referred to by many as a "sermon," given by "Miss Julia." Ben Russell said that Julia Russell's comments were "eagerly anticipated by all—some, however, with more enthusiasm than others." He elaborated that the "concerned" congregants were "most children, all owners of 'buzz-saw' outboard motors, Yankees, and other general transgressors, all easily spotted by their uneasy gazes or fixed stares—symptoms of their unwitting attempts to will way the inevitable, public condemnation of their (perceived) transgressions."

The congregation also endured irritating red bugs, known as chiggers, which lived in the pine straw. Annually, crews cleaned the Church in the Pines and replaced its benches. Ben Russell sentimentally noted in 2000 that "Church in the Pines is one of the most unique worship services in this country, and it is deeply embedded in the hearts of hundreds (four generations now) and reverently remembered by thousands." Many Lake Martin weddings and christenings were held at the Church in the Pines.

In 1963, the Dunn family donated an altar to the Church in the Pines. The altar was a memorial for William Ransom Johnson Dunn III and "all who love the lake." During the 1970s, Russell Lands, Inc., began managing the Church in the Pines, replacing the benches with permanent seating and initiating other improvements.

Seven hundred Southern Company stockholders from 33 states met at Martin Dam on May 27, 1953. Southern Company board chairman E.A. Yates selected Martin Dam as the meeting place because he thought that the site would entice many stockholders to attend. The Alabama Power Company had created the Southern Company, and the two companies had compatible agendas and shared resources. J.M. Barry, chairman of the executive committee, stated that Martin Dam was the "largest and most magnificent hydro-electric plant on The Southern Company system."

In preparation for the meeting, dam personnel and power company representatives briefed guides and hostesses about technical information concerning the dam. Landscapers prepared the grounds, and specialized professionals like nurses were available for emergencies. Some stockholders arrived in private vehicles, while many rode chartered Greyhound buses from Birmingham and Montgomery. Hostesses aboard the buses told passengers facts about Martin Dam and Lake Martin, preparing them for a tour. Stockholders gathered at the newly built reception center, which stood near the site where Martin and James Mitchell had surveyed Cherokee Bluffs in 1911 to determine whether the site was suitable for a dam and reservoir.

Participants toured the dam and grounds, enjoying the rock garden. They listened to speeches by Martin Dam superintendent Robert D. Dawkins and other dam personnel who discussed such topics as dam construction, maintenance, and safety. The stockholders learned that the dam stocked cylinders filled with carbon dioxide to protect the generators from fire during electrical system disruptions and failures. H.J. Scholz, president of Southern Services, Inc., talked about the future possibilities of atomic power.

1953 OLDTIMERS' REUNION. These lines snaked toward the barbecue tables. As tempting aromas wafted in the air, people eagerly waited to eat Lake Martin–area fish, meat, and poultry.

The meeting was successful with 82.5 percent of shares voting. Representatives of Guaranty Trust Company from New York counted the ballots. Stockholders Richard F. Carey and Nancy L. Carey from St. Petersburg, Florida, later wrote to W.M. Craven, a Southern Company industrial power division engineer in Montgomery, in which they expressed awe for Martin Dam and Lake Martin. "The location, food and atmosphere were perfect," the Careys's letter stated. They emphasized that "it was most impressive to note the gigantic scale on which the project had been carried out. It stands as a worthy monument to the foresight and ability of its creators by which the beauty of its natural setting was not marred."

The Federal Power Commission amended Martin Dam's license on December 12, 1950, to add a fourth unit. Workers built this addition to Martin Dam during 1951 and 1952, and Unit 4 opened in 1952. Dam personnel were pleased when the Gibson test of a new generator on June 14, 1953, determined that the hydraulic turbines were 93 percent efficient.

The Martin Dam and Lake Martin community hosted the third Oldtimers' Reunion of primarily former Alabama Power Company employees on October 2, 1953. Approximately 800 people arrived "from every nook and corner of the state." The power company considered anyone who had completed 25 years of employment to be an old-timer and held biennial reunions for those people. Participants either drove or rode in one of 14 chartered buses from Birmingham, Montgomery, Mobile, Jasper, Tuscaloosa, and Anniston.

CHINA PLATE. *This plate is a souvenir from the 1953 Martin Dam Oldtimers' Reunion. Every person who attended received one of these treasures.*

Dr. Tom Hagan. Dr. Hagan performed as a Native American in a 1954 skit about the history of the Lake Martin area for Tom Martin Day. Reverend Dr. Duncan Hunter, representing Alexander City's First Methodist Church, is in the background.

R.W. Kincey, a *Birmingham News* reporter, described the event as the "biggest handshaking, back-slapping gabfest Alabama has seen in many a long day." Thomas W. Martin, the oldest power company employee in continuous service, welcomed everyone, shaking as many hands as possible. J.O. Jowers, the assistant superintendent of Jordan Dam, was the master of ceremonies. Officials presented service awards. During a drawing, people won grab-bag prizes, including football tickets, tackle boxes, and other items useful for lake enjoyment. Everyone received a souvenir china plate featuring Martin Dam.

Attendees formed winding lines two city blocks long to receive a special lunch meal. The menu featured a Lake Martin taste because "there was an abundance of fried fish caught within a stone's throw from the picturesque spot." People reminisced and "Many a tall tale was told beneath the pines." The crowd listened to and cheered for both sides in the World Series broadcast in which the Brooklyn Dodgers defeated the New York Yankees.

The October 1953 *Powergrams* printed an intriguing notice. Hoyt Carlisle, senior partner of the A.C. Carlisle Drug Company, had written the power company a letter. Remarking that he had been at the Cherokee Bluffs dam construction site, he said "I

FLOTILLA SKIPPERS. They transported people to Kowaliga Beach for Tom Martin Day in 1954. Some of the men were from nearby Opelika and have beards to celebrate that city's centennial.

found a valuable item and I have reason to believe that this belongs to an employee of the Alabama Power Company working on construction of this dam." Carlisle promised, "Upon suitable evidence of ownership I will be glad to turn this item over to the proper owner." Neither Carlisle nor *Powergrams* elaborated about what the long-lost item was or if it was successfully reunited with its owner.

On July 15, 1954, Alexander City and the Lake Martin community celebrated Thomas Wesley Martin Day. That commemoration originated when Robert Russell and Sim S. Wilbanks, as representatives of a city committee, visited Martin at his home in November 1953. They told him that they wished to honor him publicly in order to show how much local people appreciated what the Alabama Power Company had developed, especially Lake Martin, to improve Alexander City and Tallapoosa County. Martin initially resisted the idea because he thought all of the people who had contributed to the projects should be recognized and not just him being singled out for praise. The members of the Alexander City committee insisted. Eventually, Martin agreed to hold an Alabama Power Company board meeting at Alexander City to coincide with the celebration.

Board members and guests arrived on a chartered Central of Georgia Railway Company train, the "Thomas W. Martin Special," which traveled between Birmingham and Alexander City. Five hundred people gathered in the city's Court Square, coming from Tallapoosa County communities and around the state to participate in the festivities. W.F. Lee led the Benjamin Russell High School Band in musical performances during the morning program, and Reverend Dr. Duncan Hunter delivered the invocation. W.R. Radney Jr., president of the Alexander City Chamber of Commerce, welcomed the crowd.

Local residents presented a five-part skit that told the history of the Lake Martin area. The actors portrayed a variety of people associated with local history, ranging from Native Americans and settlers to modern businessmen and engineers. The skit explained why and how Lake Martin was developed and how the dam and lake had advanced Tallapoosa County, emphasizing Martin's contributions. Dr. Tom Hagan and his wife performed as

Native Americans. L.E. Sellers Jr. told about a physical worker's viewpoint that electrical power reduced labor. Howard Neal stated how businessmen benefited from the lake. Mrs. J.O. Mann described how the dam and lake improved tasks for housewives, while Clarence Williams boasted, "Fishermen have taken more out of Lake Martin than they have put into it."

In his official proclamation, Alexander City mayor Joe H. Robinson declared about Thomas Martin that his "energy, resourcefulness, ability, understanding and determination" have "endeared him in the hearts and minds of the citizens of this community because of his willingness at all times to lend a helping hand and co-operate wholeheartedly in our effort at expansion." Robinson presented Martin with a silver tray. The Alabama State Chamber of Commerce president Thomas D. Russell then spoke, also praising Martin.

After the speeches concluded, a flotilla of 50 boats transported people on a 45-minute ride to Kowaliga Beach. Kowaliga Inn distributed box lunches, which people ate while enjoying the lake scenery, including the water skiers that were skimming past the shore. The day's celebration concluded with a tour of Martin Dam with people "expressing wonder at its size, the beauty of the surroundings, cleanliness of the power house."

Martin addressed the crowd, and in his speech, reminisced about his early visits to Cherokee Bluffs with James Mitchell. He recalled how they had "viewed the stream, visualized a great power dam, the storage of vast quantities of water and a state-wide power system." Martin praised Benjamin Russell's role in the creation of Lake Martin, stating that "It was shortly afterwards that Benjamin Russell and I became acquainted and from that time until his death a few years ago, we were close friends." According to Martin, Russell was "one of those few who from the start saw the great boom which would come,

KOWALIGA BEACH, 1953. These unidentified children floated with inner tubes near the beach. Playing at Lake Martin with friends was a favorite activity of area children.

WILLOW POINT COUNTRY CLUB. Many golf tournaments have been held on this golf course overlooking Lake Martin to raise money for various charities.

not alone to the County but to the people of the State, from the development of its water powers." Martin declared that Russell "foresaw the need of vast amounts of electric power; of new industry, of jobs for the boys and girls of our State."

Telling the crowd that "No honor has meant so much to me as the giving of my name to the Cherokee Bluffs dam at this site where first we dreamed that we would 'rift the hills and roll the waters' to make the lightning flash," Martin emphasized that "with all my heart I believe that what we have done is only a prologue to what the future holds." He predicted that the demand for electricity would dramatically increase as Alabama experienced more industrialization. Martin stressed that electricity would improve the quality of Alabamians' lives by "providing freedom from want, time for worship and for education, for recreation, and opportunities for self expression and the growth of personality."

Martin expressed his hopes for the advancement of the region. "The South we think of is not just a part of America; it has always been a distinctive area,—ambitious, enduring, the home of men and women who are idealists as well as practical," he said. "There is something in each of us and the history back of us that spurs us to great accomplishments in the face of adverse events," he told the crowd, "that gives us courage and the will to do the things we set out to do; something that causes us to view the future with faith." Among his goals for the Lake Martin area, Martin aspired to have the Horseshoe Bend battlefield declared a national park.

The state of Alabama and Alabama Historical Association dedicated a highway marker for the Battle of Horseshoe Bend site in 1951 on U.S. Highway 241. Hill Ferguson, chairman of the association's committee on dedication of highway markers, opened the program. Alabama Historical Association President Rucker Agee discussed events prior to the battle, and Judge C.J. Coley presented a history of the battle.

The Horseshoe Bend Battle Park Association, Inc. compiled publications such as *National Significance of the Battle of Horseshoe Bend Alabama, March 27, 1814* (1956), and the group prepared the document "Importance of the Battle of Horseshoe Bend, March 27, 1814" to submit to the United States Congress in an effort to have the battlefield designated a national military park. Congress passed the act creating the Horseshoe Bend National Military Park, and President Dwight D. Eisenhower signed it into law on July 25, 1956. This was Alabama's first national park.

On August 11, 1959, the Horseshoe Bend National Military Park opened. This federally protected site designated 2,040 acres to preserve the location of the American military defeat of Creek forces. Dedicated to both the American and Creek combatants, the park featured a visitor center and museum to educate the public about the battle, weapons, and Native American and pioneer life in the area. Hiking trails and a driving tour were created for visitors to explore and understand the battlefield.

The sesquicentennial of the Battle of Horseshoe Bend was celebrated on the anniversary of the battle in 1964 and at that ceremony, the national military park's visitor center was dedicated. The Cherokee Richard Crow, a descendant of Chief Junaluska whom the Cherokees claimed had been at the Battle of Horseshoe Bend, gave Martin an 1812 peace pipe and a certificate indicating the Oconaluftee Indian Village had adopted him as an honorary villager and named him "Lightning." Creek chief Calvin McGhee gave Judge C.J. Coley a headdress and announced that Coley belonged to the Creek tribe as "Chief Big Bear." Members of the Lake Martin community participated in a reenactment and pageant in which they represented both famous and unknown settlers

WIND CREEK STATE PARK. These two bikini-clad women boated at the park sometime in the 1960s.

and Creeks in a performance involving many dance numbers. The souvenir program, "The Day The River Ran Red," documented the area's history and included a cast list.

A 1959 *Montgomery Advertiser* article reported that "Idle Ground Developed into Tiny Coney Island" at Lake Martin—Castaway Island became a favorite lake spot. The newspaper said it had been "just a 300-acre idle hulk of real estate, jutting out like a massive three-pronged fork into the waters of Lake Martin until Cooper Crossley realized its potentialities and transformed it into the miniature Coney Island it is today." During the 1950s, Crossley and his family moved cottages, built a bathhouse and docks, and set up a miniature train ride, concession stand, and a dance pavilion that had a "mechanical waterfall" that operated when the juke box played. The Crossleys's pets, including ponies, turtles, a monkey, and a bear, which later worked as a television stand-in for "Gentle Ben," entertained visitors. People could rent paddleboats and inner tubes as well as boats. Lifelong Lake Martin resident Jim Bain Jr. exclaimed, "Castaway WAS Lake Martin!"

Palmer Taylor, who had poured concrete piers for the Kowaliga Bridge, remained in the lake area and was intrigued by its possibilities. By 1960, Taylor and his son Teddy leased land from the Alabama Power Company to open a store for lake residents and visitors. Walking across the property, they thought the experience was "like exploring a lost world. From beneath the thick underbrush peeked chimneys from old homeplaces, old roads, even remains of an old blacksmith shop." Teddy even rescued his father once when he stepped into an obscured well. While they began building in spring 1961, an "early flood that year filled the lake to levels never before seen." The Taylors worked all winter, keeping fires burning so that newly poured concrete would not freeze. A store, docks, and fuel tanks were set in place. The Taylors named it Real Island Marina to remember the

WIND CREEK CAMPSITES, 1968. Tents were popular shelters for Lake Martin camping at this time.

RACING ROWING TEAMS. In May 1969, the Dartmouth College and the University of Alabama in Huntsville rowing teams raced on Lake Martin.

Real family that had once lived there. Real Island Marina became a favorite picnic and reunion site. An icehouse held huge blocks of ice that employees crushed and placed in paper sacks for customers. Rental apartments, floating docks, and boat storage sheds were also available, and the marina's Shell sign was a familiar lake landmark.

In 1961, Russell Corporation created Russell Lands to develop lakefront properties for residential communities and recreational venues. Owning 300 miles of Lake Martin's shore, Russell Lands expanded into Alabama's largest recreational developer, and the firm has thrived and grown in the decades since its establishment. Its headquarters overlook Lake Martin. Because the company oversees timberlands around the lake, over the years it has harvested and sold some wood for industries to use as steam generation fuel.

Developed by Russell Lands, the Willow Point Country Club opened in 1965. Here, golfers could play on greens overlooking Lake Martin. That course hosted the Boy Scout Pro-Am golf tournament since 1975. Russell Lands sold waterfront lots at Willow Point in addition to later recreational developments called Riverbend and Windermere.

Initially a Russell development, Wind Creek State Park first admitted visitors in 1961. The Wind Native Americans had lived there, and then farmers, including Sid Hertzfeld, lived on that land. A plaque honoring Robert A. Russell was formally dedicated five years later on September 3, 1966, and in 1971, the state of Alabama purchased the land to use as a state park. Featuring a marina, docks, and store, the 2,000-acre Wind Creek park also provided a 210-foot fishing pier for anglers. The campground was built with over 600 sites, some of which were by the lake so that boats could be kept at campsites. Hiking trails, playgrounds, pavilions, and sandy beaches provided lake visitors of all ages with recreational options. The grain silo that Hertzfeld built was used as a gift store, then as Park's Nature Museum, becoming the park's landmark. Visitors could climb to the silo's

LAKE MARTIN BEACH.
Women relaxed on a Lake
Martin beach while their
families played in the water.

top to view a panorama of lake activity. Educational programs were offered to teach people about trees, wildflowers, and wildlife living at Lake Martin. Hiking guides led people along the lake's ridges and shorelines. Lake resident Toppy Hodnett, who had developed Kowaliga, was commissioner of Conservation and Natural Resources for Governor George Wallace and secured $5 million to improve Wind Creek State Park, which was closed from 1979 to 1981.

In 1963, the National Campers and Hikers Association held its convention at Wind Creek State Park with 600 families participating. Wind Creek is best known for hosting numerous fishing tournaments; it has a weigh station to determine precise measurements before fish are released in the lake. Fishing guides often included Wind Creek on trips, saying that its lake waters attracted fish. During the 1960s, the lake was stocked with almost 1 million striped bass. The State Conservation Department attempted to stock salt water striped bass in Lake Martin in the late 1960s. Largemouth, spotted, white, and hybrid bass also formed large lake populations, in addition to catfish, sunfish, crappie, and bluegills. Every March and April, striped and white bass migrate to spawn in shoals at Hillabee Creek and on the river channel near the northern lake shore. In the summer, striped bass live closer to the dam and as deep as 80 feet in order to keep cool. Fishermen can bass fish at Lake Martin year-round.

In addition to Wind Creek, other recreational sites were developed to meet different users' needs. For example, the Alabama Power Company and the Maxwell and Gunter Air Force Bases developed recreational facilities for military personnel to boat, fish, camp, and picnic. The Police Youth Camp, Inc. and Bama Park with its blue slide were opened. Camp Talisi hosted Boy Scouts from nearby communities as well as from Opelika, Montgomery, and Birmingham. The Seventh Day Adventist Church established Camp Alamisco at Blue Creek in 1968.

Alabama governors George Wallace and Lurleen Wallace owned a Lake Martin cabin during their gubernatorial terms in the 1960s. The lake provided them a retreat to relax, savor friendships with trusted people, and devise political strategies. Lurleen Wallace was an avid angler since childhood and fished as often as she could while campaigning for her husband or herself or governing the state. She often spent time at lakes near campaign stops or political rallies to fit in fishing, and Lake Lurleen at Northport was named in her honor. She also enjoyed deep-sea fishing off the Alabama Gulf Coast.

Mr. And Mrs. Fred Rea were the Wallace's Lake Martin neighbors and friends. They hosted a Lake Martin picnic for Lurleen Wallace's campaign workers after she won the Democratic nomination in the May 1966 primary. While Governor George Wallace lounged in a hammock, reading newspapers, Lurleen Wallace indulged in recreational activities. A talented boat operator, she drove a speed boat and assisted water skiers. Lurleen Wallace enjoyed showing off by skiing with two skis then kicking one off before she began to slalom.

Lurleen Wallace most enjoyed fishing at Lake Martin and catching its bass. *Birmingham Post-Herald* outdoor writer Ray Veasey remarked that Lurleen Wallace "enjoyed all types of

WATER RECREATION IN LAKE MARTIN. Heads bob above the lake as people cool off in Lake Martin on a hot summer day.

fishing, lantern fishing at night and tight line and trolling. If fish were biting, she refused to quit for lunch or even to rest." Veasey occasionally fished at Lake Martin and observed Wallace fishing. According to Veasey, "Often she would don her overalls, fill her thermos bottle with coffee, and fish off by the pier for stripes." He noted that Lurleen Wallace baited her own hook and was capable of pulling out fish of all sizes. Sometimes she sat on her pier until after midnight, holding her fishing pole to practice. The Wallace pier had a live-well basket that she had constructed and which was often full of fish during her fishing sessions. Wallace also fished from a boat she paddled into a slough, saying she liked this method "where I could get a little fishing done and get a tan at the same time."

In an April 7, 1968 *Birmingham News* article, Newman revealed that a number of prominent Alabamians owned Lake Martin homes, including Auburn University presidents Dr. Ralph Draughon and Dr. Harry Philpott and University of Alabama president Dr. Frank Rose. College football coaches Paul "Bear" Bryant and Ralph "Shug" Jordan also had lake cabins.

> Coach Jordan and Coach Bryant have entertained just about the entire families of the Southeastern Conference. Paul and Mary Harmon entertain Alabama football writers every year. They have had as their guests Bud Wilkinson, Duffy Daugherty, John McKay, Darrell Royal, Jim Owens, Charley Bradshaw, plus members of the Sugar, Orange, Liberty, Cotton, Gator and Bluebonnet Bowls. During the filming of the Coach Bryant ABC special, which was shown to more

BOY SCOUT TROOP 7. These Tallassee Boy Scouts raised the American flag at Martin Dam on July 4, 1972. Pictured are Danny Hunter, Bobby James, and Michiel Torbert.

SOUTHBOUND GLORY. This bluegrass band performed at the Still Waters Arts and Crafts Show in 1977.

than 40 million, Paul and Mary Harmon hosted the ABC narrators, script writers and photographers. And only Carney Laslie could help the Bear barbecue the three-inch steaks.

In 1969, the Alabama Power Company prepared a report to petition for the Martin Dam license to be renewed when it expired on June 8, 1973. The Federal Power Commission had the option to renew the license, issue it to a new licensee, or take control of the dam. The illustrated report provided technical details and historical commentary as evidence that the Alabama Power Company should continue operating Martin Dam. "The Company respectfully submits that the public interest would be served best by the issuance of a renewal license to Alabama Power Company containing appropriate terms and conditions," the report asserted, claiming "that a takeover of Martin Dam by the United States or issuance of a new license to a new licensee would not be in the public interest."

The power company emphasized that the "generating capacity at Martin Dam is used primarily to help supply the peak load requirements imposed by the public on the interconnected electric system of Alabama Power and the other companies in The Southern Company system pool." Alabama Power carefully maintained and updated the dam. New technology installed at the dam included frequency system relays to minimize outages and new governors to permit control from Birmingham. The power company also asserted its role in creating a valuable recreational site: "To say that Martin Lake is beautiful is to make a gross understatement—for nowhere else is there a more inviting area, steeped in Indian lore, for fisherman, boater, bather, water skier, camper, and nature lover."

DRYING OFF. Lisa Schafer, Laura Haak, Cristina Rodriguez, and Mauricio Rodriguez dry off after exploring Lake Martin in the summer of 1978.

On April 21, 1969, Alabama governor Albert P. Brewer wrote to Gordon M. Grant, secretary of the Federal Power Commission in support of the Alabama Power Company's license to operate Martin Dam be continued. Brewer stated that "Martin Lake (F.P.C. Project Number 349) located on the Tallapoosa River in Alabama is one of Alabama's most popular recreational attractions." He noted that the lake "is extensively used not only by the citizens of our State but by visitors from all over the country." Brewer concluded by emphasizing that "This lake, created by Alabama Power Company's construction of Martin Dam in 1926, has been so developed through the years by the Company and by other private interests that it now offers to all visitors a veritable water wonderland."

Area residents formed the Lake Martin Resource Association in the late 1960s. Ben Russell recalled that the "first primary mandate at that time was to convince Alabama Power Company and the Federal Regulatory Commission that something had to be done about the unstable and sporadic lake levels which were evident on our lake prior to the early 70's." Also sometimes referred to as the Lake Martin Recreation Association, the group united people to create a secure, hospitable environment at the lake. Their projects, including buoy placement, CPR training, and boating safety, impacted the lake for decades.

Near the former community of Susanna, the Still Waters golf course was completed by 1972 when construction for the Still Waters Resort and Conference Center was initiated. This gated community was carefully planned to cater to residents and vacationers. Spread over 2,200 acres, Still Waters has expanded over the years to offer a variety of leisure activities and services, including tennis courts, lounges, and a fitness center. The Church of the Living Waters at Still Waters provides services and ceremonies by the lake. The Harbor House Convention Center is a meeting place for events and socializing, and residents and visitors can choose fine cuisine or casual foods from menus. The resort has a full-service marina for boaters and a pro shop for golfers playing on Still Waters's two nationally acclaimed courses, the Legend and the Traditional. People can purchase or rent houses, villas, or condominiums.

The lake was the center of an overwhelming amount of activity. National champion water skier Freddy Hardwick, who won titles in 1966 and 1970, was from Lake Martin. The Kowaliga Ski Club (later named the Lake Martin Ski Club), Dixie Sailing Club, and Still Waters Yacht Club staged tournaments and regattas. Fiberglass boats became more common on the lake's waters. Lake Martin became a popular site for family and class reunions and football parties. Alternating floods swelled the lake, and droughts depleted it.

Some Lake Martin area residents were deployed to Vietnam, and that conflict contrasted dramatically with the peaceful atmosphere of the lake. People supported the servicemen, both past and present. In 1972, Major Lemuel P. Montgomery, the first

CAMP ASCCA. These campers rowed a canoe on Lake Martin. Fun water activities help children develop skills and enhance self-confidence.

American Horseshoe Bend casualty, was moved from the Dudleyville cemetery to Horseshoe Bend National Military Park. At Montgomery's Horseshoe Bend burial services, the National Muzzleloading Rifle Association presented a rifle salute, and the Tohopeka chapter of the Daughters of the American Revolution placed flowers on his grave. That organization had erected a gravestone for Montgomery at Dudleyville in 1933. United States senator John Sparkman and Representative Bill Nichols attended. Horseshoe Bend was included on the National Register of Historic Places in 1976.

Jackson Bostwick, who played the original Captain Marvel on the television show *Shazam!* in the early 1970s, often visited Lake Martin as a child. His parents, Dr. Jackson Leonard Bostwick and Mary Elizabeth Bostwick, rented a Russell cabin at Willow Point beginning in 1958. The younger Jackson Bostwick remembered, "At that time Willow Point Country Club and Golf course was a cow pasture; Acapulco Rock was graffiti free." He claimed to have "put up the first giant rope swing at Chimney Rock" with friend Bruce Jordan and "often night-fished under old Kowaliga Bridge with a Coleman lantern." Bostwick recalled that he and his sister June performed water skiing stunts for the neighboring Governor Wallace's amusement. He also guided Lurlene Wallace "to the best fishing holes in her favorite slough." In the 1980s, Bostwick established the L.A. (Lower Alabama) Film Group, Inc. at the lake.

Therapeutic efforts associated with the lake began with the formation of Camp ASCCA (Alabama Special Camp for Children and Adults), the world's largest camp for handicapped people. In 1974, Camp ASCCA, affiliated with Easter Seals, was built on Lake Martin at Jackson's Gap. Two years later, 323 campers attended the first session. Camp ASCCA representative Phil Martin said that sporting activities, especially water sports, challenged campers. He explained that "it's really a big self-esteem booster for them to get out there and do something they've never done." One camper praised Camp ASCCA because, for the first time, "I was seen as an individual and not as a chair." Camp Civitan was held at Camp ASCCA.

By 1975, the old Kowaliga bridge was replaced with a modern bridge. The Game and Fish Division of the Alabama Department of Conservation and Natural Resources convinced the state highway department to save the spans near the shores to convert the old bridge into fishing piers. Its rubble formed an artificial reef, and fishermen considered that site a good place to catch crappie.

Harper Lee, the Pulitzer Prize–winning author of *To Kill a Mockingbird*, visited Lake Martin in the 1970s. She was researching a local murder in which a voodoo preacher was slain.

Hurricanes Eloise in 1975 and Frederic in 1979 crossed the Lake Martin area. The latter hurricane "dumped so much rain into the lake that all the gates and generators were wide open," a tour guide said. "Water thundered—3,016,000 gallons per minute through each spillway—and spray rose up into the air blotting out the dam." Joanne C. Walker, writing for *Lake Martin Living*, recalled that the "pounding river chewed huge bites, still obvious, our of the red mud banks and the cracking of trees as they fell sounded like gunshots. Visitors poured in to watch this awesome phenomenon."

7. Luxury and Leisure: Home at Lake Martin in the 1980s and 1990s

During the late twentieth century, Lake Martin became much more than a vacation spot or temporary retreat for many people. The 1980s and 1990s witnessed the construction of more elaborate, expensive luxury houses and condominiums as investors and retirees flocked to Lake Martin. Thousands of retirees decided to make Lake Martin their permanent home. Also, people from nearby towns chose to live in a home at the lake and commute to work. People renovated weekend cabins into larger houses with sufficient room to meet daily needs for cooking, entertaining, and living. The Alabama Power Company and Russell Lands owned most of the lake's undeveloped land. Much of the power company land was made into subdivisions. Russell Lands created more elaborate properties. Huge mansions and designer houses were built and featured in such magazines as *Southern Living, Southern Accents, House and Garden*, and *Builder/Architect*. Property values dramatically increased as exclusive residential developments were created.

Although housing prices soared, retirees were attracted to Lake Martin because related living costs were among the most affordable in the United States. Alabama property taxes were extremely low; Tallapoosa County property tax is .35 mils. Retirees found Lake Martin's rural setting appealing, calming, and safe, and they found the mild climate agreeable. Retirees realized that urban resources, including hospitals, airports, universities, and shopping centers, were within reasonable driving distances. The immediate Lake Martin community offered opportunities to participate in civic, philanthropic, cultural, social, volunteer, and religious activities. Accessibility to satellite and internet services in the 1990s connected Lake Martin to the world. Lake Martin attracted a variety of people, including Barbara Mandrell who hosted an area golf tournament.

In 1989, the Alabama Advantage for Retirees, a state-sponsored program to evaluate how to attract retirees, focused on the Lake Martin and Alexander City area. The assessors concluded that Lake Martin had "everything necessary for ideal retirement." During the 1990s, national magazines included Lake Martin in lists of the United States' best retirement communities. In August 1992, *Kiplinger's Personal Finance Magazine* described the Lake Martin area as one of "Ten Retirement Spots That Feel Like Home." Peter

Dickinson in the 1992 book supplement *Sunbelt Retirement* rated Lake Martin as "excellent." Two years later, *Where to Retire* magazine selected the Lake Martin area as "One of America's 25 Most Affordable Retirement Towns," "One of America's Best Neighborhoods for Active Retirees," and "One of America's Top Five Area's for Military Retirees." The August 8, 1994 *Wall Street Journal* named the Lake Martin community number one of "Ten New Retirement Spots."

The July 24, 1995, *Fortune* magazine retirement guide issue described Lake Martin as a "Retirement Haven" for its availability of the "Most Affordable Housing." David Savageau picked the Lake Martin area as first in the housing category and eighth in the money matters category in the 1995 edition of *Retirement Places Rated*. Lake Martin was the subject of the "Undiscovered (retirement) Haven" feature published in the Winter 1997 *Where to Retire* magazine. During the 1990s, Russell Lands became the state's major private recreational developer, and that corporation excelled in attracting retirees to Alabama. "Who's Who in Luxury Real Estate" included Russell Lands in its exclusive directory. Various Lake Martin souvenirs, including Lake Martin Santa ornaments and T-shirts promoted the lake.

In July 1987, the first issue of *Lake Martin Living* was published. Editor Jim Bain Jr. told readers that the magazine's objective was "To present a true, interesting insight into the life we all love, 'Lake Martin Living.'" Bain belonged to a prominent Lake Martin family whose boaters and water skiers were nationally acclaimed. He stated, "We really did have lake water in our blood." *Lake Martin Living* offered readers a feast of information about lake personalities, events, and history, and the magazine presented full coverage of lake competitions and events. Bailey Jones's column, "Growing Up," was a favorite feature that many readers read first. *Lake Martin Living* began sponsoring writing and photography contests in 1993, with categories including people, lake scenes, wildlife, and miscellaneous

WIND CREEK STATE PARK. These people are enjoying playing horseshoes. Members of Triskaideks Alabama Good Sam Chapter frequently camped at Lake Martin.

CAMP ASCAA. These two unidentified campers delighted at being towed in an inner tube. Being splashed by refreshing Lake Martin water was a welcome treat.

for pictures, and history, memories, fishing and boating stories, ghost stories, and children's favorite activities at the lake for writing. A business that would later become significant to *Lake Martin Living*, Dale Broadcasting, Inc., began airing the radio station WZLM (Lake Martin)/Z-97 in 1989.

The Lake Martin community elaborately celebrated the Fourth of July. Former United States postmaster general Winton Blount and his wife Carolyn, who have a vacation home at Lake Martin, sponsored fireworks for many years. In 1988, the Lake Martin First Annual Independence Day Flag Boat Parade at Kowaliga was held and became an anticipated tradition.

Wind Creek State Park underwent renovations during the 1980s and was designated as Alabama's largest camping park. Scheduled activities included fishing tournaments and the annual Lone Eagle's Pow Wow, which began in 1994 to feature Native American crafts and activities.

Children attended a variety of camps in the Lake Martin area. Camp ASCCA hosted day camps for local children. Girls camped at Kamp Kiwanis sponsored by the Girl Scouts. St. James School in Montgomery brought its fifth graders annually since 1996 to Camp ASCCA for a science camp. Students learned about aquatic organisms, testing water quality, forestry, wildlife, and how to use a compass. "The teaching of environmental stewardship is greatly needed in Alabama," Dan Gilliland, Camp ASCCA program director, said. "Our mission with science camps is to promote the idea and practice of 'stewardship' rather than 'ownership' of our environment." Camp Civitan, founded in the 1970s for mentally disabled people, was transferred to Camp ASCCA in 1994 and renamed Camp Civitan of Easter Seals. The Alabama Elks Youth Camp began operating at Lake Martin in 1999. In 1997, the Alabama Power Company built the D.A.R.E. Power Park, a public recreational site, by Young's Landing.

CHILDREN'S HARBOR. This peaceful Lake Martin site offers people a relaxing outdoor atmosphere to cope with serious illnesses.

Marinas taught boating safety classes to help boaters pass licensing tests. Dixie Sailing Club built a clubhouse on the Kowaliga Basin and hosted boat races. Boaters could also join the Still Waters Yacht Club and participate in regattas. The Po' Ol' Kowaliga Regatta was a favorite fundraiser for Children's Harbor that consisted of races and auctions. The Lake Martin Ski Club offered facilities, instruction, and competition.

Lake Martin area writer Dorothy Baughman wrote a romance set at a lake based on Lake Martin, and Avalon Books published her *Ghost of Aronov Point* in 1980. In Baughman's novel, the main character Marcy Pemberton is a lifeguard at Walker Lake in Alabama who falls in love with the wealthy Benjamin Aronov.

In the 1980s, Greg Cecil, owner of Cecil's at the Lake restaurant, restored the Kowaliga statue, which had been vandalized. Many Lake Martin people referred to that establishment as Kowaliga Restaurant.

Children's Harbor, a sanctuary for critically ill or injured children, was built at the lake near the Kowaliga Bridge. Ben and Luanne Russell planned Children's Harbor in 1987, emphasizing that its "sole purpose is to strengthen children and families." The buildings and land were dedicated in 1990 to Adelia McConnell Russell. Children's Harbor at Lake Martin was created as a partner to the Children's Harbor Family Center at Birmingham's Children's Hospital. Many of those patients travel to Lake Martin as a retreat during their treatment. Young visitors enjoyed camp sessions, while their parents could relax knowing their children were having fun at a place where suitable medical and emotional support was available.

The Children's Harbor grounds have several Lake Martin landmarks. Plymouth Lighthouse, located on Providence Point, symbolizes Children's Harbor's "goal of helping children and families through the treacherous and troubled waters in which they sometimes find themselves." Children's Harbor personnel stressed, "We believe that our services to children and families must be God-centered and firmly grounded in spiritual values." The Children's Harbor Chapel is representative of the "picturesque New England seaside village motif," and other buildings include Harbor House, cottages, and administrative headquarters. The adjacent section of Elmore Highway 63 was named Our Children's Highway.

Children's Harbor hosted free camps for children with various illnesses. Camp Smile-A-Mile included children undergoing cancer therapy in addition to children who survived treatment for five years. According to camp personnel, "The kids off therapy are an inspiration to those currently on treatment and they can share experiences." Participating in traditional camp activities such as sports and crafts, campers stay at Lake Martin for one week. The camp's purpose is "to provide these children with avenues for fellowship, to help build self-confidence, to help them cope with their disease, and to prepare them for life." Day and weekend trips for educational, cultural, or sporting events are also scheduled, and family camp sessions help people coping with a recent cancer diagnosis. Parents and siblings accompany campers to Children's Harbor and participate in counseling to learn how to nurture sick children. "Having a child with a chronic illness is like living in a war zone," a father divulged. "It is so good to come to a place where you can find hope for a normal life."

Several thousand children have attended the Mariners' Adventure Camp annually since 1991. This camp was established "so children with special needs could attend camp and have the same happy childhood memories as other children." Campers could enjoy activities such as boating that they had not previously experienced due to medical

CHILDREN'S HARBOR CHAPEL. This chapel provides solace to Lake Martin residents and visitors.

concerns. They also bonded with counselors and other children, which was significant because they had often been isolated while undergoing treatment. Other camps were held for transplant and burn victims, Magic Moments recipients, and mentally handicapped people. Children's Harbor also hosts able-bodied campers who are unable to afford camps. The Mariner's Adventure Course offers groups, including athletic teams and business executives, the chance to develop teamwork skills.

In 1987, Luanne Russell agreed to coordinate services at the Church in the Pines across the road from Children's Harbor. Two years later, Russell Lands gave the church to Children's Harbor. Services were held at the Church in the Pines from Memorial Day to Labor Day, then at Children's Chapel during the rest of the year. Nearby, a large time capsule was buried in Time Capsule Park in 1989. This container commemorated "The Year of the Child" and was scheduled for opening in the year 2039.

Although jet skis were common, residents enjoyed the annual antique and classic boat and car show to raise funds for Children's Harbor and traditions such as the Christmas Boat Parade, featuring boats decorated with lights. The Sarah Towery Art Colony at Children's Harbor sponsored an annual workshop and festival.

The August 10, 1988 *New York Times* printed future Pulitzer Prize–winner Diane McWhorter's article, "The Call of the Lake Is Music to Southern Ears." She told readers that the "Friday-afternoon cry of 'Let's go to the lake!' defies the work week pressures of efficiency and progress wrought by promoters of the Sun Belt." She revealed some of the lake lingo she overheard, including "How far down is the lake?" and "hit it!" McWhorter observed that "The ability to start behind the boat on one ski after getting up on two, is the badge of the lake achiever. 'Can you get up on one?' is the challenge of the lake." She described "Chimney Rock [as] a 70-foot cliff below which boats converge in a perpetual

RELAXING AT THE LAKE. Pictured here are Sally Robertson Hall, Sally Robertson Wood, and Beverly Robertson Webster, who frequently visited with each other at their families' Lake Martin houses.

LAKE MARTIN. This panoramic scene shows a typical weekend as people gather at favorite sites to catch up with friends after a long work week.

floating traffic jam." In the late 1980s, the Alabama Power Company estimated that Lake Martin had 2.68 million annual visits. McWhorter noted that Saturday evenings were the lake's busiest social events and that

> This summer, Mr. Russell has been sponsoring the most coveted of Saturday-night entertainments: moonlit cruises on the *Love Thy Neighbor*. Mr. Russell built this lakeworthy hottub and equipped it with a carousel horse and what he calls "a hellacious P.A. system" that blares "our theme song" Clarence Carter's "Strokin."

She observed, "For the lake people, local color is Sunday lunch at the Talisi Hotel, an old-fashioned home-cooking establishment in a picturesque mill town down the Tallapoosa." After eating, McWhorter observed, "There is more dock-hopping and water-frolicking, as consensus builds on staying over until Monday morning." McWhorter concluded her piece by mentioning a Montgomery banker's wife telling singer Paul Simon, "You mean you've never been to Lake Martin? . . . Oh, you must come."

On Halloween night 1988, Blan Stewart disappeared near Lake Martin. A Huntsville insurance agent charged with mishandling more than $500,000 of client money, Stewart had rented a Piper Archer airplane before he was reported missing. State and federal authorities investigated whether Stewart faked his death and fled to another country to escape prosecution. Because Stewart's whereabouts were unknown, his survivors were denied $4 million of his life insurance. Search crews from A&T Recovery, a Chicago company, sent scuba divers to Lake Martin because residents reported hearing a plane the night Stewart disappeared. Four other underwater recovery groups had previously searched the lake. Scuba divers located Stewart's airplane on November 16, 1990, with sonar equipment. The airplane had been snared in trees 65 feet deep near Bama Park and Chuck's Marina. Stewart's body was inside.

An October 14, 1990 program, "The Land and the Lake: Tallapoosa County and Lake Martin," was held at Pebble Hill in Auburn. This meeting sponsored by the Auburn

WIND CREEK STATE PARK. These visitors Alan and Edna Montgomery, founding members of Triskaidas Alabama Good Sam Chapter, were on their way to visit friends nearby.

University Center for the Arts and Humanities featured speakers, including Ben Russell, Ben Hyde, Dr. Charles Farrow, Judge C.J. Coley, Mary Lee Carter, and Elizabeth Wright Strother. They presented historical accounts and personal experiences of life in the region.

Lake Martin continued embracing the military, and many residents were retired officers. Area servicemen fighting in the Gulf War received community support. Parts of the sunken World War II B-52 bomber that crashed into Lake Martin were salvaged in 1992. Bob Norwood of Montgomery dedicated time to researching and finding the bomber to answer mysterious questions that had puzzled the Lake Martin area for decades. At the time of the crash, people heard what sounded like an explosion near Sandy Creek. Foresters found pieces of an airplane and contacted Maxwell Air Force Base, which had reported a bomber was missing. Because of the war, the military was vague about the missing airplane and its mission.

Fascinated by the Lake Martin bomber mystery since he was a teenager, Norwood sought newspaper, military, and historical information. As an adult, he began looking for the plane's location in the lake in 1990. Norwood determinedly searched the Sandy Creek area, using a military map from the crash report and depth finder. With friends Jeff Norris and Bruce Edwards, he laid out a grid of buoys. Frustrated because they were not having luck, the men realized that the plane crashed when the water level was low. As a result, they revised their search and saw something on their depth finder. During a dive at that site, Norris found a piece of the bomber. They realized that the aircraft was in 6 feet of mud beneath water 50 feet deep.

The trio stopped diving so that Norwood could determine how to proceed. Reluctantly, the Air Force gave Norwood legal rights with the provision that if the two men missing in action were recovered he would notify military officials. Norwood then acquired permission from the Alabama Power Company and the Alabama Historical Commission to pursue salvaging the bomber. In the summer of 1992, Norwood and his colleagues retrieved the plane's tail section, which had been broken during the military's salvage efforts. They also found the propeller, a fire extinguisher, and a wheel part.

Charles Oliver Jr., the son of one of the missing crew members, called Norwood about his salvage work and provided Norwood details about his father that had not been released publicly. The bomber had crashed because one of the engines had exploded and was on fire during a storm. Smoke poured into the plane, disorienting its crew. Possibly, the plane may have turned upside down from the impact of the explosion because that was the position in which it was found.

Oliver also participated in dives at the crash site, and the men found fragments from the airplane, as well as a dress shoe. Norwood later retrieved the bomber's two engines. As time, money, and technology allowed, he devoted himself to cleaning mud off of the bomber in the hope that he would eventually wench it out of the lake and restore it, possibly even fly it someday, in an on-going process continuing through to the present.

Devoted to the lake, residents continued to ally in the grass roots effort, the Lake Martin Resource Association (LMRA), to protect the environmental quality of the lake, conserve natural resources, and defend the lake's existence during the "water wars" with Georgia, which wanted to drain water from the portion of the Tallapoosa River in that state for drinking supplies. Members could discuss lake issues and concerns and participate in committees. The association's newsletter *Lake Lines* featured safety, environmental, fish and wildlife, water quality, and security issues. The first Lake Martin environmental

1988 DROUGHT. *This water was so low in the summer that area residents commented that Lake Martin resembled its usual winter appearance.*

forum was held on July 18, 1992. The Lake Martin Resource Association negotiated with the Alabama Power Company and the Federal Energy Regulatory Commission to set a lake level plan, referred to as the "rule curve," to set acceptable level ranges. The group sponsored Annual Lake Martin Lake Clean-Up sessions, gathering tons of trash. The LMRA put hazard buoys in Lake Martin and sponsored boating safety classes with the lake's Marine Police.

In 1991, the Lake Martin chapter of PALS (People Against a Littered State) formed to beautify the lake. On October 12, 1991, volunteers removed trash from the lake's shore and roadsides. Real Island residents raised funds to create a volunteer fire department in 1991, and they planned to buy a fire boat because most of Lake Martin's homes were accessible by water.

The 1986 and 1988 droughts, the March 1993 blizzard, and Hurricane Opal in October 1995 all altered the lake's landscape. Opal downed so much timber that the Alabama Power Company estimated, "Opal's aftermath won't soon be forgotten. It could take more than 20 years for the company to replace the volume of timber lost to the storm." Wet weather and demands on logging crews slowed cleanup.

On the afternoon of June 12, 1993, a sudden storm assaulted Kowaliga Marina. Hail and wind destroyed the roof covering one dock and piled boats on top of each other and the dock. Pines trees slammed into the Kowaliga restaurant. Sadly, Jack T. Anderson Sr. of Birmingham suffered a heart attack when his pontoon boat capsized during the storm; he later died.

1993 BLIZZARD. Snow blanketed the Lake Martin area and some residents enjoyed the opportunity to sled.

In September 1996, the last remnants of the old Kowaliga bridge were demolished. Transportation Department divers examined the remaining wood bridge pilings, describing the bridge's support posts as being rotted and "dangling in the water." Some fishermen unsuccessfully attempted to save what they considered a valuable fishing pier. Workers used a crane to load bridge pieces on a barge that would take them to a site to form an underwater reef. During the dismantling process, bridge timbers broke, and Frank D. Williams and Randall L. Phillips fell from the pier where they were working and were fatally trapped by collapsing bridge debris.

In 1998, local entrepreneurs envisioned the idea for a business organization, then chartered the Lake Martin Area Economic Development Alliance. The alliance aspired to attract businesses to the Lake Martin area through a program of promoting the community in a variety of media. The alliance sought coordination with community leaders, governments, schools, and agencies to develop appealing incentives to recruit businesses and industries. The Lake Martin Area Economic Development Alliance recognized that "Those businesses that currently exist in the Lake Martin area are its most vital asset and the backbone of our economy." As a result, the alliance sought to retain those businesses by identifying issues such as infrastructure and workforce training, which need to be improved for economic growth to occur.

Built in 1998, the Lake Martin amphitheater by the Big Kowaliga Basin united the community with Easter sunrise services, bluegrass festivals, and concerts by performers such as Jett Williams and Ricky Skaggs. Russell Lands, Inc. created the amphitheater for

KOWALIGA STATUE. *The statue was in peril before firemen rescued it. Onlookers shouted to relief workers to save this beloved Lake Martin icon.*

135

KOWALIGA RESTAURANT. *A 1999 fire destroyed the restaurant. The sudden blaze surprised area residents, who rushed to the site in an attempt to save this treasured Lake Martin landmark.*

public events, which are overseen by the Lake Martin Arts Council and all profits contributed to Children's Harbor. In 1987, Ben Russell had arranged for the site to be clear cut and replanted. He ordered crews to cease planting when he realized what a spectacular view existed there. The amphitheater debuted with a 1999 Easter sunrise service. Russell envisioned improving the site with expanded seating, a covered stage, and dance floor. He also hoped to use the site for orchestras, Shakespeare performances, ballets, and historical reenactments.

A June 1999 fire razed the Kowaliga Restaurant owned by Russell Lands. The front page of the June 19, 1999 *Montgomery Advertiser* printed photographs of firefighters and the restaurant. At 9:30 on the morning of the June 18, Tae Buckhanon, an employee at the Kowaliga Kubbard grocery store near the restaurant, smelled smoke and gas. She called the nearby Kowaliga Marina to report that the restaurant was on fire. The Red Hill Volunteer Fire Department and surrounding communities' firefighters quickly responded. People gathered around, including restaurant renter Greg Cecil, who helplessly watched his business burn. Observers yelled for the firefighters to save the Kowaliga statue. The firefighters dragged Kowaliga to safety. He had minor fire damage where plastic had melted. Several firefighters suffered from heat exhaustion as they struggled to put out the fire. Charles Chambers remarked, "The restaurant's gone, but we saved the Indian."

Also in June 1999, sophomore University of Georgia golfer Reilley Rankin seriously injured her back after jumping off Chimney Rock. She had been national freshman of the year, a first-team All-American, SEC Golfer of the Year, and had won the SEC championship. Rankin missed the 1999–2000 golf season while recuperating from a fractured sternum and vertebrae. The injuries occurred when she hit Lake Martin on her back after leaping 70 feet from Chimney Rock. Auburn golfers Courtney Swaim and Anne Hutto had taken Rankin at the lake to boat and relax. Georgia coach Beans Kelly stated, "There's a 30-foot [rock] and a 70-foot [rock] and Reilley wanted to go to the top right away." Kelly noted that "It was probably more dangerous for her to climb back down than to jump. Unfortunately, she just landed wrong." Rankin was taken to the University of Alabama at Birmingham's Medical Center for rehabilitation.

Lake Martin has been the site of local, regional, and national fishing competitions. Annually, Lake Martin was selected as a Bass Anglers Sportsman Society (B.A.S.S.) Tournament Trail site. The first BASSMASTER tournament at Lake Martin was held from December 6 to 9, 1989, with sleet and snow pelting competitors. Robert Tucker from Houston, Texas, won with fish totaling 53 pounds and 11 ounces. Wayne Waldrop from Alexander City won the amateur division of that tournament with 24 bass totaling 30 pounds and 15 ounces. Top competitive fishermen at Lake Martin included Trip Weldon from Wetumpka who placed second at the BASSMASTER Eastern Invitational tournament in 1999 after competitively fishing at the lake since 1978. Pete Gluszek from

REPAIRING MARTIN DAM. These two Alabama Power Company employees belonged to crews repairing Martin Dam in 1995.

New Jersey won that tournament. Tennessean Charlie Ingram won the BASSMASTER Top 100 Pro-Am tournament in 1990, and Mike Terry, also from Tennessee, won the BASSMASTER BP Top 100 in 1993. Lady Bassers competed in a tournament at Still Waters in March and April 1992.

Steve Price wrote about Lake Martin for *FalconGuide, America's Best Bass Fishing*. He stated that the "joy of fishing Lake Martin is not knowing what you've caught until you see it, for this is probably the best lake in Alabama, as well as one of the better lakes in the South, for catching both quality largemouth and spotted bass." Price noted that the two bass species often could be found together in Lake Martin unlike in other lakes. Commenting that heavy bass were often caught, he recalled a 1989 professional bass tournament at Lake Martin "in which the winner boated more than 53 pounds of fish."

Tackle designer Charlie Brewer used Lake Martin to test new products, including his Slider light tackle fishing system. He was able to catch more than 50 fish daily while testing his prototypes. "I have to rank Lake Martin right at the top of my list of favorite lakes because of the sheer number of fish it has," Brewer said.

In 1993, the Alabama Power Company and Bass Anglers Sportsman Society fishermen created artificial reefs consisting of Christmas trees that were sunk near Pace's Point. Area grocery stores provided collection sites for people to donate their trees. Volunteers then bundled and weighted the trees to sink these fish-friendly habitats. The United States Corps of Engineers granted permission for the power company and BASSMASTERs to recycle trees as reefs, and the Alabama Department of Conservation and Natural Resources helped because this project reduced landfill surpluses after Christmas. Some Lake Martin fishermen privately placed artificial reefs.

The Alabama Power Company's Corporate Real Estate division used draft horses to remove trees without damaging adjacent land. Horses, unlike machines, only pulled out selected timber, and their hooves did not tear up sod the way machinery tires did. Chief forester Bennie Vinson commented that the power company's methods left property

ARTIFICIAL REEFS. Recycled Christmas trees were submerged to form artificial reefs. Only a few weeks before, these Christmas trees proudly decorated Lake Martin homes.

GOAT ISLAND. *Many herds of goats have called this Lake Martin island home. Boaters hope to glimpse the lake's famous goats when they pass by the island.*

intact because people remained aware that the land was wooded and not stripped or clear cut. "The forestry section operates under a multi-use concept for company-owned lands," Vinson explained. "We're trying to maintain a healthy forest that is productive, not only for growing timber products, but for recreational purposes such as hunting, fishing, and the ownership of houses on leased lots of company land around the lakes."

New developments often incorporated history. When Lock and Beverly Hunter built their house in the Trillium development, they asked architect Don Stansell how to design the house to co-exist with Tecumseh's Rock, which was on their lot. Russell Lands insisted that the boulder remain on the property because of its historical significance to the lake area.

Water quality is also an important issue at Lake Martin, which is considered one of the cleanest and most attractive in Alabama. The non-profit Lake Watch of Lake Martin was formed in 1991 by residents wanting to pursue proactive methods to preserve and improve the ecological quality of the lake's water and expand public awareness. Colonel Dick Bronson leads much of the Lake Watch work. Cooperating with the Alabama Department of Environmental Management, Alabama Water Watch Program, Auburn University, and governments, Lake Watch volunteers were the state's first trained water quality monitors as of 1993. Lake Watch focused on scientific studies of lake water, legislative activities, and educational programs to discourage pollution and harmful activities detrimental to water quality. The group was concerned with the safety of drinking water and how it influenced public health.

At designated sites, volunteers collected monthly water samples to test for E. coli bacteria and aquatic organisms, such as benthic macroinvertebrates, and compiled data measuring oxygen, temperature, alkalinity, and other chemical concerns. Lake Watch's free Living Streams program taught children and adults how to evaluate water quality with hands-on experiences gathering and analyzing specimens from Lake Martin at Camp ASCCA. This work led to winning science fair projects, such as that prepared by Elmore County student Hope Middleton. Foreign visitors, often associated with Auburn University's fisheries department, visited Lake Martin to learn about Lake Watch's programs. The Tallapoosa Watershed Task Force was developed to identify pollution sources, such as agriculture, industry, recreation, and lakefront property.

Collection sites include Horseshoe Bend Military Park, Coley Creek, Elks Lodge, Raintree/Sugar Creek, Bay Pine Island, Smith Landing, Alamisco, Still Waters, and Kowaliga. "When my husband and I travel to our water test site on Lake Martin, we pass a hand-painted sign tacked to a pine tree that reads: 'Go on God's errands,' " volunteer monitor Dr. Kathryn Braund said. "That pretty well sums up Lake Watch for us. We believe it is our responsibility to honor and protect the Creator's work through careful stewardship. We must protect it from present threat and preserve its beauty and goodness for future generations."

During the 1990s, Lake Watch was involved in the "water wars" between Alabama and Georgia. This conflict concerned how water should be allocated to communities from the Alabama-Coosa-Tallapoosa River basin. In order to secure more drinking supplies for Atlanta and its expanding suburbs, Georgia officials planned to build the West Georgia Regional Reservoir on the section of the Tallapoosa River in that state. This action would have diverted water flowing southwest to Lake Martin. At least 22 percent of the lake's 3,000-square-mile watershed is located in Georgia. The West Georgia Regional Reservoir would control 8 percent of the lake's Georgia watershed. Lake Martin also was threatened by other reservoirs being built on the Tallapoosa and Little Tallapoosa Rivers in Georgia. Lake Watch emphasized how water quantity and water quality were linked in an effort to stop reservoir developments north of Lake Martin. That group asserted that water released from northern Tallapoosa River reservoirs might be polluted because of the large population areas the water serviced. Lake residents also became aware of the needs of Montgomery and Auburn for additional water resources and the possibility that Lake Martin might be tapped for those communities.

State Representative Jack Venable restocked Goat Island with a herd of African pygmy goats in 1998. Auburn University veterinary students monitored the herd and provided worm blocks to eliminate parasites. The goats attracted visitors from throughout the United States and Europe. Unfortunately, the goats were killed and replaced with another herd that only lived on the island for five months before they were killed. "Thousands of children and families derive great pleasure each summer by visiting the goats, watching them, and feeding them," Larry Bennett, who placed the goats on the island, said. "If this is not stopped, it will be the last chapter in a long tradition of enjoyable activities our beautiful lake offers residents and visitors," he warned. "I urge the Lake Martin Community to assist in every way to stop this senseless string of reckless and irresponsible acts resulting in the killing of these pets who really belong to the whole Lake Martin Community."

8. Questions and Answers: The Twenty-First Century

The Lake Martin community continued to grow in the early twenty-first century. Residents, visitors, and developers planned for the future based on their hopes and aspirations for lake living and recreation. The community also dealt with adversity, both local and national. State Representative Betty Carol Graham told the *Alexander City Outlook* for an article printed on January 26, 2000, that "Water is something that is taken for granted. The Tallapoosa River and Lake Martin are the economic salvation for the county in the times we are in now."

In 2000, Children's Harbor published *The Church in the Pines Hymnal*, which contains Ben Russell's history of the church and both religious and patriotic songs. Each song provides credit information for the composer and lyricist and sometimes the creation date or a comment if a psalm inspired the music. The song "The Church in the Wildwood" reminds listeners of the Church in the Pines.

The former Kowaliga Restaurant was rebuilt in August 2000. Now called Sinclair's Kowaliga, the restaurant displays Hank Williams's albums on its walls, and Kowaliga returned to greet patrons by the door. Customers can eat inside or outside and enjoy panoramic views of the lake. Boaters can park their watercraft at slips the restaurant's dock.

In summer 2000, Lake Martin experienced one of Alabama's worst droughts. The National Weather Service said that the drought was the longest that had occurred in Alabama for a century. Because rainfall was 10 to 20 inches below normal, the lake level dropped, and people were warned to use the lake carefully because boats might get snagged or stuck in shallow water. Alabama Power Company representatives reminded people at Lake Martin that the lake's water was essential to maintain power generation and to keep river levels navigable. *Lake Martin Living* advised boaters to steer clear of shallow spots and move closer to the river channel. "If your neighbor's water access is in worst shape than yours—help him out—offer him the opportunity to use your dock," the magazine urged. "That's one thing Lake Martin has always been known for—its friendly people. So let's show it."

Sam Wade replenished Goat Island with ten goats in June 2000. A watch group was established to protect the goats from being poisoned or shot. Lake Martin residents and visitors were reminded that the Alabama legislature had passed legislation declaring

KOWALIGA STATUE. Kowaliga stands guard at Sinclair's Restaurant on the site of the former Kowaliga Restaurant.

animal cruelty crimes were felonies. Visitors were asked not to bring dogs onto the island to prevent attacks on the goats. The watch group also recorded hull numbers of campers' boats to report littering violators.

Governor Don Siegelman named Wind Creek State Park to the Alabama Bass Trail in October 2000. "The establishment of the Alabama Bass Trail is the most practical way to enhance our economic impact," he stated, and "to draw national attention to our natural treasure while improving our facilities and fisheries." Siegelman hoped the Alabama Bass Trail would "showcase to the world what this great state has to offer." Wind Creek improved its infrastructure with new floating docks and staging area to weigh in fish.

During late 2000, workers replaced 60 arches over the spillway gates in the dam because their concrete was deteriorating. Most of the arches were from the original dam construction. A spillway gate had arches facing upstream and downstream and in the middle. Workers used a crane placed on a barge that also carried supplies. The tugboat *Miss Imogene* transferred materials between the barge and shore.

In November 2000, Dale Broadcasting, Inc., the operator of WZLM/Z-97, published its first issue of *Lake Martin Living*. The new owners explained that "Earlier this year we started looking for a way to grow our company and allow us to do an even better job of promoting Lake Martin and bring the lake communities together as one." They stated, "As longtime friends and admirers of *Lake Martin Living* magazine we decided that this would be a natural way for us to grow." The magazine changed from a "home based business to an 8 to 5 establishment with a staff of employees."

Donna Burkett began editing and publishing a glossy magazine filled with readers' contributions and stunning photographs taken by Tim Phillips. Former editor Jim Bain Jr.

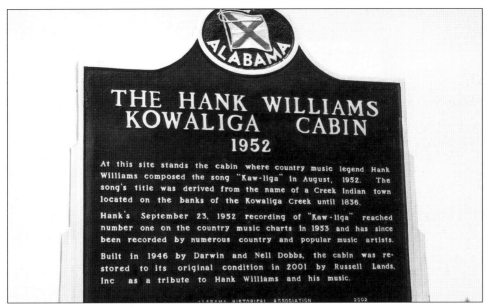

THE HANK WILLIAMS KOWALIGA CABIN

1952

At this site stands the cabin where country music legend Hank Williams composed the song "Kaw-liga" in August, 1952. The song's title was derived from the name of a Creek Indian town located on the banks of the Kowaliga Creek until 1836.

Hank's September 23, 1952 recording of "Kaw-liga" reached number one on the country music charts in 1953 and has since been recorded by numerous country and popular music artists.

Built in 1946 by Darwin and Nell Dobbs, the cabin was restored to its original condition in 2001 by Russell Lands, Inc as a tribute to Hank Williams and his music.

HANK WILLIAMS SR. HISTORICAL MARKER. In 2002, the Alabama Historical Association recognized this site as significant to Lake Martin's and Alabama's heritage.

told readers, "It's time for *LML* to go to the next level to better serve both the advertisers who support it and our legion of faithful readers." He reassured people that the new "owners are local business people who have either grown up in the Lake Martin area or who have become enthralled with its beauty since locating here." Bain stated, "These are 'lake people' like myself who love the area and want to see it prosper in the right way. Their heart is in the right place."

Lake Watch announced in December 2000 that Alabama and Georgia were nearing agreement on a Alabama-Coosa-Tallapoosa (ACT) water allocation proposal to submit for federal evaluation. "One major roadblock to final approval of an ACT agreement is the important linkage between our river basin and the Appalachicola-Flint-Chattahoochee (ACF) River Basin," the Lake Watch newsletter reported. The group hoped for resolution of all the water-related conflicts, but admitted, "Although the ACT proposal is light-years ahead of previous ones, there are still some problems with it, particularly as it affects the Tallapoosa River Basin and Lake Martin."

An angler caught a white crappie that was of state record size in April 2000, and fishermen continue to devote time to studying fish patterns and learning where the best places to fish on Lake Martin are located. Their strategy in competition is to catch largemouth bass that increase the total weight of the five-fish limit. Droughts can be problematic, but heavy rainfall has usually restored Lake Martin to competitive levels.

In December 2000, the Alabama BASSMASTER Eastern Invitational was held during three days at Lake Martin. Approximately 325 anglers from 26 states, Canada, and Mexico competed. Jimmy Millsaps placed first, catching fish weighing 13 pounds, 24 ounces. Winners received part of a $232,000 purse and points qualifying anglers to compete in the elite BASSMASTERs Classic, which bass fishermen consider their sport's Super Bowl. Only four 2001 tournaments awarded points to make five anglers in the Eastern category eligible for the summer BASSMASTERs Classic. B.A.S.S. Angler of the Year Tim Horton said, "Lake Martin is unique in that you can get down in clear water and catch bass deep or you can get in stained water and catch them shallow."

In March 2001, Takahiro Omori won the Wal-Mart Forrest L. Wood (FLW) tournament at Lake Martin's Wind Creek State Park in a field of 346 fishermen from 34 states and Japan. This victory was Omori's first on the professional bass tour. Skillfully working crankbait to catch the competition's limit, he received $100,000 after catching five bass totaling 10 pounds, 14 ounces in the final five-man round. "I can't believe it," Omori told the *Alexander City Outlook*. "When I started out fishing the FLW Tour five years ago, I couldn't really speak English and I was camping out to get by. Now, I've finally made it." Four other professional Japanese fishermen competed in the tournament due to an international angler exchange. *Outdoor Life* writer Mike Jone profiled Omori and other Japanese competitive anglers, referring to them as "The Samurai Bass Masters."

ESPN covered the tournament, presenting live broadcasts. "Many contestants struggled with the rapidly changing lake conditions brought about by a series of cold fronts and thunderstorms that swelled Lake Martin by more than 4 feet in the last week," the *Alexander City Outlook* reported, "leaving the upper end of the lake rolling red with mud and sediment. Snow even fell on the 40,000-acre impoundment during Tuesday's last minute practice session." During the Wal-Mart competition, Willie White became the first African-American angler to win a bass tournament when he won the $15,000 Co-Angler Division. Two-time FLW Tournament winner Rick Clunn remarked about the Lake

PATRIOTISM AT LAKE MARTIN. Many people watched the Fourth of July fireworks show from boats on Lake Martin.

ADVERTISEMENT FOR BOATS. Over the decades, area merchants have advertised products, such as these motors featured in a 1950 Alexander City Outlook *ad, to help boaters win races on Lake Martin.*

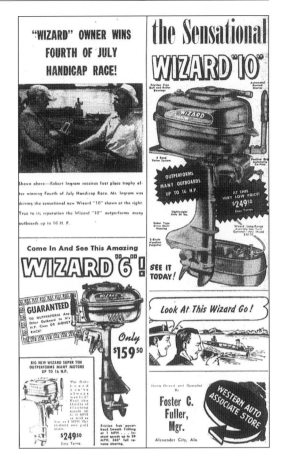

Martin competition, "Most of the guys are going to catch their limit." As a result, he stated "You need one of the big ones to put you over the top."

The Alabama legislature passed a law, effective in 2001, that raised the age for operating watercraft. The law also lowered blood alcohol levels for boating under the influence convictions. "My constituency utilizes the recreational benefits of Lake Martin year round," State Senator Ted Little said. "This legislation will create a much safer environment and bring forth a better quality of recreational benefits on Lake Martin and throughout all of Alabama." Little emphasized, "I am pleased to have been a part of supporting this bill in the state senate."

During the summer of 2001, crews transported log cabins to the amphitheater grounds. These cabins formed the nucleus of a pioneer village. Russell Lands assumed sponsorship of the Fourth of July fireworks show, which Red Blount had hosted through 2000. The Fourth of July fireworks was moved to the amphitheater "so family and friends can celebrate our nation's birthday Lake Martin style." Many people watched the show from boats on Lake Martin.

After the September 11, 2001 terrorist attacks, Martin Dam was closed to the public except by appointment. The dam was identified as a potential target for sabotage, either

145

MARINAS AND REALTORS. Both services advertise on Lake Martin street corners. These signs help visitors locate businesses on twisting roads along Lake Martin's shoreline.

through physical or cyber attack. In summer 2002, federal authorities warned of potential hacking of the dam's computer controls. Several Lake Martin residents traveled to New York City and Washington, D.C. to help recovery efforts. *Lake Martin Living* printed reflections and poems addressing how the tragedy had affected people at Lake Martin. Aware that the "moon in 'my' sky is the same moon that shines on Afghanistan, Pakistan and Saudi Arabia," Connie Montgomery wrote, "I ask myself a lot of questions here in the cool darkness and I wait for answers to come."

The October 30, 2001 *Birmingham Post-Herald* reported that Vulcan, the city's landmark 56-foot-tall iron statue, sculpted by Giuseppe Moretti to depict the god of fire and forge, was visiting the Lake Martin area as an "honored guest" for repairs. Crews initially transported approximately 40,000 pounds, about one-third of Vulcan, on flatbed semi-trucks from Vulcan Park in Birmingham to Alexander City. The remaining parts of Vulcan were moved in early 2002. Robinson Iron Corporation in Alexander City cleaned, stripped rust-red lead paint, painted with pewter-colored finish, patched cracks, and restored Vulcan. The base pieces were examined first, according to Scott Howell, general manager of Robinson Iron, who told the *Birmingham News* that "We will be able to crawl around inside these pieces and study them closely to get accurate measurements from our engineers." The god's torch was replaced with a spear point. Workers created some parts that had disappeared since Vulcan was erected in 1904 and recast broken pieces. Alexander City Chamber of Commerce executive director Susan Foy commented that residents

LAKE MARTIN CORNER. Here, signs and artifacts, such as the pink flamingo, tell visitors which cabins are located on each slough.

were pleased that Vulcan was vacationing near the lake and wished he could stay instead of returning to Birmingham. "We could put him on Lake Martin and let him overlook all of the boaters," she said.

On January 4, 2002, the *Montgomery Advertiser* reported that Elmore County commissioners requested state legislators to consider funding a feasibility study for a 30-mile outer loop between Interstates 65 and 85 connecting Elmore and Montgomery Counties. The officials emphasized that this route would aid commuters and encourage businesses to locate in Elmore County because of easier interstate access. Thomas Coram, mayor of Eclectic, suggested that the proposed loop should "swing north of Eclectic and Lake Martin" because the "future of Elmore County is in Lake Martin."

In 2002, Russell Lands returned the Darwin and Nell Dobbs' cabin from Pitchford Hollow to its original location near Kowaliga to transform it into a museum. Luanne Russell decorated the restored cabin. Using photographs taken about the time Hank Williams Sr. stayed there, Russell recreated the interior to duplicate the images in the photographs, including the decorative plates, card table, alarm clock, bottle opener, and ukulele. David Mitchell, a Hank Williams enthusiast, urged the Russells to undertake this project. The Dobbs's cabin had been incorporated into Percy and Thelma Yergan's cabin. On June 22, Jett Williams stayed at the cabin when she came to Lake Martin for her "Stars Fell on Alabama" amphitheater concert. She delighted in remembering how her parents had enjoyed spending time at the cabin. The Alabama

Historical Association placed a historical marker on the highway by the cabin site on the Children's Harbor grounds.

Children's Harbor sponsored Time Capsule Park by the Kowaliga Bridge, and on February 17, 2000, a large steel canister, resembling a rocket, was filled with artifacts and buried in Time Capsule Park. The Children's Harbor Year 2100 Time Capsule contained a computer with a CD preserving photographs of Lake Martin taken in 2000. School children contributed personal photographs, letters to descendants, toys, and prophecies about what they thought might happen during the twenty-first century. Scrapbooks with genealogies were included in addition to civic and community documents and publications. Materials chronicling Children's Harbor were placed in the time capsule prior to argon gas pressurizing the tube. The Year 2001 capsule was then encased in an underground cement block in the same field as "The Year of the Child" time capsule. "I think it will be interesting to our descendants to see what Children's Harbor is doing now," executive director Jim Ray remarked, "and how our services will evolve over the next hundred years."

On March 11, 2002, Children's Harbor hosted its first Market Day, an annual event created to raise money for Children's Harbor. Vendors sold crafts, furniture, books, food, and other items at what resembled a large yard sale or flea market. Live musical

ANTIQUE BOAT AT CHILDREN'S HARBOR. People flock to the docks to admire old-fashioned boats at this fundraiser for Children's Harbor.

ANTIQUE BOATS AT CHILDREN'S HARBOR. People often congregate at Harbor House and the bell house for special events at Children's Harbor.

performances entertained patrons. The Children's Harbor's new mascot Big Ben and puppets amused visitors. Children were given balloons and played games on the grounds. Boats were displayed in the lake.

In spring 2002, Auburn Kiwanis build a gazebo for Camp Smile-A-Mile, a Children's Harbor camp specifically for cancer treatment survivors. The Lake Martin Resource Association placed new "Take Pride in Lake Martin" road signs around the lake. That group also discussed lake levels with the Alabama Power Company. The Lake Martin Resource Association wanted lake levels to be dropped later in the fall and raised earlier in the spring to improve recreational use of the lake. Association president Ben Russell reminded people that the lake's and dam's purpose was for flood control. He commented, "I believe that the original license for Martin Dam had provisions for 60-foot drawdowns, and the lake has been down 50 feet in my lifetime." He said that the Federal Energy Regulatory Commission determined lake level and flood control guidelines.

The "water wars" negotiations continued in the early twenty-first century. Georgia changed its reservoir site to Beech Creek, but Alabama water resources were still impacted. United States Representative Bob Riley said that "counties east of Birmingham—the congressional district I represent—are expecting a strong industrial boom in the coming years and will need the water more than ever before." He admitted, "True, the river systems have their headwaters in Georgia, but their downstream waters are the life-blood of most parts of Alabama, and it has been that way for many, many years." Jim Campbell, Alabama's main negotiator, and Willard Bowers, Alabama Power Company's hydropower head, spoke at the 2001 annual Lake Martin Resource Association meeting at the Church in the Pines. Campbell told listeners that the water agreement in December 2000 was acceptable because "We got everything that we had to

MISS LAKE MARTIN, 1977. The Miss Lake Martin Pageant continues to be held annually to crown a local beauty, such as 1977 winner Cheryl Clements, to represent Lake Martin at the Miss Alabama pageant.

have" and most "of the things that we wanted." Bowers said the power company was considering shortening the duration of low water levels each year. Ironically, the level of Lake Sidney Lanier near Atlanta dropped so much in summer 2002 that many Georgians flocked to Lake Martin with their boats in order to persue water recreation activities.

Jett Williams performed annually at the Lake Martin Amphitheater during the early twenty-first century. She told the crowd, "This is sacred ground. Dad came to write here and escape here." The third Jett Williams Kowaliga Reunion, rescheduled and held on August 17, 2002, was called "Stars Fell on Alabama." Williams encouraged Lake Martin residents to participate in a live recording for an album during the concert and celebrate the 50th anniversary of the writing of "Kaw-Liga." In addition to Williams, Razzy Bailey, Freddie Hart, Hank Locklin, Han Adam Locklin, and Jeanne Pruett were scheduled to sing.

Local beauties vied to become Miss Lake Martin (formerly the Miss Still Water pageant) and to qualify for competition at the Miss Alabama pageant. Some young women also competed in the annual Bay Pine Bikini Contest.

Still Waters offered Cabins on the Green and Condominiums on the Lake. The Ridge Marina opened in May 2001, and the ribbon cutting for the River North Marina was held two months later. Auburn coach Tommy Tuberville and his wife Suzanne enjoyed a 7,000-

square-foot house in Marina Marin. Decorated with Auburn tiger motifs, the house hosted Auburn fans and athletic department personnel. Sometimes the Tubervilles watched the Auburn swim team practicing in Lake Martin while their coach monitored them from a boat.

The lake inspired creativity. Pat Cunningham Devoto wrote her novels, *My Last Days as Roy Rogers* and *Out of the Night that Covers Me*, at her Lake Martin home. Lake Martin's treasured storyteller, Bailey Jones, published 37 of his *Lake Martin Living* columns, "Growing Up," in volume 1 of *Growing Up: Tales About Life on the Lake*. Ron and Dale Drinkard's Lake Martin house was included on the New York Museum of Folk Art's southeastern tour. Their house is decorated with paintings and pieces created by significant folk artists.

Although it is no longer the world's largest artificial lake (Uganda's Owen Falls still held that honor as of 2002), Lake Martin elicits glowing praise from local residents and visitors. Fishing guide Doug Patterson stated, "I have lived on or near Lake Martin all my life and wouldn't want to live anywhere else in the world." *Alexander City Outlook* and *Dadeville Record* publisher Bruce Wallace said what so many people feel about the lake when he declared, "Lake Martin is the jewel in the crown that is the Alexander City-Dadeville Area." Reminiscing about Benjamin Russell and Thomas W. Martin, Ben Russell urged, "Their vision is in our hands, let's make Lake Martin a repository for the dreams of the past and those of the future."

LAKE MARTIN GEESE. Geese always welcome a friendly gift of food. Whenever this child visits her grandmother's Lake Martin cabin, she asks for bread to feed the geese.

Appendix

Martin Dam Tour: 1 (800) 525-3711

The Alabama Power Reservoir Information System: 1 (800) LAKES11

Lake Martin Marine Police: (256) 234-2601

Alabama Marine Police: 1 (800) 272-7930

Lake Martin Fishing Information:
http://www.dcnr.state.al.us/agfd/fish/lake/martin.html

Dixie Sailing Club: http://www.dixiesailingclub.com

Lake Watch: P.O. Box 72, Alexander City, AL 35011. Phone: (256) 825-9353. Fax: (256) 825-1873. http://www.lakewatch.org

Alabama Water Watch publications including Lake Martin:
http://www.auburn.edu/aww/awwprogram/publications.htm

Lake Martin Resource Association: 2544 Willow Point Road, Alexander City, AL 35010. Phone: (256) 329-0835 ext. 355. Fax: (256) 212-1453

Lake Martin Area Economic Development Alliance: P.O. Box 1105, Alexander City, AL 35011. Phone: (256) 215-3725. Fax: (256) 215-3760. http://www.lakemartinalliance.com

Lake Martin: http://www.lakemartin.com (This site contains information ranging from the location of boat launches to current water levels.)

Lake Martin Living: P.O. Box 909, Alexander City, AL 35011. Phone: (256) 825-4221

Adelia M. Russell Library: 318 Church Street, Alexander City, AL 35010. Phone: (205) 329-6796

Dadeville Public Library: 203 N West St, Dadeville, AL 36853-1301. Phone: (205) 825-7820

Horseshoe Bend Regional Library: 207 N West Street, Dadeville, AL 36853-1355. Phone: (205) 825-9232

Tallassee Community Library: Corner of Central Blvd (Highway 14) and Freeman Street, P.O. Box 308, Tallassee, AL 36078. Phone: (334) 283-2732

Town of Eclectic Library: 137 Old Salem Rd, Eclectic, AL 36024-6435. Phone: (334) 541-3228

Alexander City Chamber of Commerce: P.O. Box 926, Alexander City, AL 35011. Phone: (256) 234-3461

Dadeville Area Chamber of Commerce: 185 South Tallassee Street, Dadeville, AL

36853. Phone: (256) 825-4019. http://www.dadeville.com. E-mail: chamber@lakemartin.net

CAMP ASCCA: P.O. Box 21, Jacksons Gap, AL 36861. Phone: (256)825-9226, 1 (800) THE CAMP

CHILDREN'S HARBOR: 1 Our Children's Highway, Children's Harbor, AL 35010-9534. Phone: (334) 857-2133. http://www.childrensharbor.com

WIND CREEK STATE PARK: 4325 AL Hwy 128, Alexander City, AL 35010. Phone: (256) 329-0845. Fax: (256) 234-4870

RUSSELL LANDS INC.: 2544 Willow Point Road, Alexander City, AL 35010. Phone: (256) 329-0835. http://www.russelllands.com

STILL WATERS RESORT: 1000 Stillwaters Road, Dadeville, AL 36853. Phone: (256) 825-7021

KOWALIGA MARINA: 255 Kowaliga Marina Road, Alexander City, AL 35010. Phone: (334) 857-2111. http://www.kowaligamarina.com

SINCLAIR'S KOWALIGA: 295 Kowaliga Road, Alexander City, AL 35010. Phone: (334) 857-2889

REAL ISLAND MARINA: 2700 Real Island Road, Equality, AL 36026. Phone: (334) 857-2741

HORSESHOE BEND NATIONAL MILITARY PARK: 11288 Horseshoe Bend Road, Daviston, AL 36256-9751. Phone: (256) 234-7111. http://www.nps.gov/hobe/index.htm

THE HANK WILLIAMS MUSEUM: 118 Commerce St., Montgomery, AL 36104. Phone: (334) 262-3600. Fax: (334) 262-0686. E-mail: HankWilliamsMus@aol.com. http://www.hitdude.com/hank.html

FREE PUBLIC ACCESS BOAT RAMPS

Alexander City Boat Ramp (city owns)
Baker's Bottoms Ramp (Alabama Power Company owns)
D.A.R.E. Power Park Ramp (Alabama Power Company owns)
Jaybird Landing Ramp (Alabama Power Company owns)
Madwin Creek Ramp (Alabama Power Company owns)
New Hope Church (county owns)
Paces Point Ramp (Alabama Power Company owns)
Piney Woods Landing (county owns)
Smith Landing Ramp (Alabama Power Company owns)
Sturdivant Creek Ramp (Alabama Power Company owns)
Union Ramp (Alabama Power Company owns)

ALABAMA FISHING AND BOATING REGULATIONS

http://www.dcnr.state.al.us   1 (800) 432-7389

State law requires all boat operators to be licensed. Anyone 12 or older can receive a boater's operating license by passing an Alabama Marine Police written examination. Children younger than 12 cannot operate boats or any type of individual watercraft on

Alabama's public waters. Boaters have to be 14 or older to boat alone.

Out-of-state boaters must follow boating regulations of their home state. They can boat in Alabama for 45 days before an Alabama license is legally required.

The Boating Under the Influence law cites a .08 blood alcohol content as legally drunk for adults. People under 21 face zero tolerance. Anyone arrested for boating while intoxicated while transporting minors younger than 14 aboard the boat will have his or her penalties doubled.

Owners of motorized boats are required to register them at probate offices or courthouses and affix boat license numbers on each bow side in order to operate on Alabama waters.

Every person in a watercraft must wear a Personal Floating Device (PFD).

There are specific requirements for boats towing water skiers and operating at night or when visibility is poor.

Alabama Power Company issues lake maps printed with specific rules for safe and courteous boat operation, information about standard lake markings, swimming and water-skiing safety guidelines, and hazards to boaters operating near the dam.

Alabama residents from 16 to 65 years old are required to purchase a state fishing license from sporting good stores, marinas, bait shops, convenience stores, or courthouses. Fees vary according to license duration and for fresh or saltwater fishing. Fishing licenses can also be combined with hunting permits.

Alabama Power Company Shoreline Guidelines

Because the power company owns Lake Martin's pool property and is concerned with shoreline management, specific activities, particularly lakefront construction, require site review by a power company representative; examination of documentation, including deeds, property surveys, and project plans including proposed materials; official approval; and issuing of permits prior to construction. Some developers also have standards with which owners must comply. Guidelines provide specific instructions and address construction and placement of the following: boathouses, boatslips, floating structures, piers, ramps, satellite dishes, seawalls, wetslips.

Alabama Power Company phone numbers to arrange appointments for construction review:

(205) 825-4002, (205) 825-0053, (205) 257-2810

BIBLIOGRAPHY

RESOURCES

Adelia M. Russell Library, Alexander City
Alabama Department of Archives and History, Montgomery
Alabama Power Company Corporate Archives, Birmingham
Auburn University Archives and Special Collections, Auburn
Horseshoe Bend Regional Library, Dadeville

PERIODICALS

Alabama Sportsman
The Alexander City Outlook
Birmingham Age-Herald
Birmingham News
Birmingham Post
Dadeville Spot Cash
The Eclectic Observer

Lake Martin Living
Lake Martin's Homes and Land
Montgomery Advertiser
Montgomery Journal
Powergrams
The Tallapoosa News
The Tallassee Tribune

BOOKS AND ARTICLES

Adair, James. *The History of the American Indians*. Edited by Samuel Cole Williams. London: Charles Drily, 1775; reprint ed., New York: Argonaut Press, 1966.

Adams, George I. *Gold Deposits of Alabama and Occurrences of Copper, Pyrite, Arsenic and Tin*. University, AL: Geological Survey of Alabama, 1930.

Andrews, Johnnie. *Fort Toulouse Colonials: A Compendium of the Colonial Families of Central Alabama, 1717-1823*. Introduction by John Sledge. Prichard, AL: Bienville Historical Society, 1987.

Benton, Jeffrey C., comp. *The Very Worst Road: Travellers' Accounts of Crossing Alabama's Old Creek Indian Territory, 1820–1847*. Eufaula, AL: Historic Chattahoochee Commission, 1998.

Brannon, Peter A. *The Southern Indian Trade, Being Particularly a Study of Material from the Tallapoosa River Valley of Alabama*. Montgomery, AL: The Paragon Press, 1935.

Braund, Kathryn E. Holland. *Deerskins & Duffels: Creek Indian Trade with Anglo-America, 1685–1815*. Lincoln: University of Nebraska Press, 1993.

Brewer, George Evans. *History of Coosa County*. Montgomery: Alabama State Department of Archives and History, 1955.

Clayton, Lawrence A., Vernon James Knight Jr., and Edward C. Moore, eds. *The De Soto Chronicles: The Expedition of Hernando de Soto to North America in 1539–1543*. 2 vols. Tuscaloosa: University of Alabama Press, 1993.

Cline, Wayne. *Alabama Railroads*. Tuscaloosa: University of Alabama Press, 1997.

Cobb, Hubbard. *American Battlefields: A Complete Guide to the Historic Conflicts in Words, Maps, and Photos*. New York: Macmillan, 1995.

Corkran, David. *The Creek Frontier: 1540–1783*. The Civilization of the American Indian Series, No. 86. Norman: University of Oklahoma Press, 1967.

Crist, James F. *They Electrified the South: The Story of the Southern Electric System*. Published by author, 1981.

Debo, Angie. *The Road to Disappearance: A History of the Creek Indians*. Norman: University of Oklahoma, 1941.

Dryden, Charles W. *A-Train: Memoirs of a Tuskegee Airman*. Tuscaloosa: University of Alabama Press, 1997.

Eggleston, G.C. *Red Eagle and the Wars with the Creek Indians of Alabama*. New York: Dodd, Mead & Co., 1878.

Escott, Colin, with George Merritt and William MacEwen. *Hank Williams: The Biography*. Boston: Little, Brown, 1994.

Ferguson, Harley B., William M. Black, and William T. Rossell. *Reports on Examination and Survey of Etowah, Coosa, Tallapoosa and Alabama Rivers (Georgia and Alabama)*. Washington, D.C.: Government Printing Office, 1914.

Florette, Henri. *The Southern Indians and Benjamin Hawkins, 1796–1816*. Norman: University of Oklahoma Press. 1986.

Foscue, Virginia O. *Place Names in Alabama*. Tuscaloosa: University of Alabama Press, 1989.

Galloway, Patricia, ed. *The Hernando de Soto Expedition: History, Historiography, and "Discovery" in the Southeast*. Lincoln: University of Nebraska Press, 1997.

Ghioto, Paul A., Mark E. Spier, and Faye Johnson. *Facts, Legends and Accounts of the Battle of Horseshoe Bend*. Daviston, AL: Horseshoe Bend National Military Park, 1979.

Golden, Virginia Noble. *A History of Tallassee for Tallasseeans*. Tallassee: Tallassee Mills of Mount Vernon-Woodberry Mills Inc., 1949.

Graves, Fannie Martin. "History of Elmore County through 1876." M.S. thesis. Alabama Polytechnic Institute, 1937.

Green, Michael D. *The Politics of Indian Removal: Creek Government and Society in Crisis*. Lincoln: University of Nebraska Press, 1982.

Griffith, Benjamin W. Jr. *McIntosh and Weatherford, Creek Indian Leaders*. Tuscaloosa: University of Alabama Press, 1988.

Halbert, H.S., and T.H. Ball. *The Creek War of 1813 and 1814*. Montgomery, AL: White, Woodruff, and Fowler, 1895.

Heidler, David S., and Jeanne T. Heidler. "Between a Rock and a Hard Place: Allied Creeks and the United States, 1811-1814." *Alabama Review* 50 (1997): 267–289.

————. *Old Hickory's War: Andrew Jackson and the Quest for Empire*. Mechanicsburg, PA: Stackpole Books, 1996.

The Heritage of Tallapoosa County, Alabama. Clanton, AL: Heritage Publishing Consultants, Inc., 2000.

Hooper, Johnson Jones. *Adventures of Captain Simon Suggs, Late of the Tallapoosa Volunteers: Together With `Taking the Census' and Other Alabama Sketches.'* Introduction by Johanna Nicol Shields. Library of Alabama Classics republication of the 1858 edition. Tuscaloosa: University of Alabama Press, 1993.

Hornady, John R. *Soldiers of Progress and Industry*. New York: Dodd, Mead & Co., 1930.

House, Jack. *Lady of Courage: The Story of Lurleen Burns Wallace*. Montgomery: League Press, 1969.

Hudson, Charles. *The Southeastern Indians*. Knoxville: University of Tennessee Press, 1976.

Ingram, William P. *A History of Tallapoosa County*. Birmingham: W.P. Ingram, 1951.

Jackson, Donald C. *Great American Bridges and Dams*. Washington, D.C.: Preservation Press, 1988.

Jackson, Harvey H. III. *Rivers of History: Life on the Coosa, Tallapoosa, Cahaba, and Alabama*. Tuscaloosa:University of Alabama Press, 1995.

————. *Putting "Loafing" Streams to Work: The Building of Lay, Mitchell, Martin, and Jordan Dams, 1910–1929*. Tuscaloosa: University of Alabama Press, 1997.

Kelley, Jennie Lee. *Alexander City Centennial, 1874–1974*. Alexander City: Alexander City Centennial Celebration Committee, 1974.

Knight, Vernon J. Jr. *Tukabatchee: Archaeological Investigations at an Historic Creek Town, Elmore County, Alabama, 1984*. Tuscaloosa: Office of Archaeological Research, Alabama State Museum of Natural History, University of Alabama, with the cooperation of the Alabama Development Office, 1985.

Knight, Vernon J. Jr., Gloria G. Cole, and Richard Walling. *An Archaeological Reconnaissance of the Coosa and Tallapoosa River Valleys, East Alabama, 1983*. Moundville, AL: University of Alabama, Office of Archaeological Research, 1984.

Koon, George William. *Hank Williams, So Lonesome*. Jackson: University Press of Mississippi, 2001.

Ledbetter, Kenneth T. "Lake Martin Sailboat Marina." B. Arch. thesis. Auburn University, 1980.

Martin, Joel W. *Sacred Revolt: The Muskogees' Struggle for a New World*. Boston: Beacon Press, 1991.

Martin, Thomas W. *Forty Years of Alabama Power Company*. New York: Newcomen Society, 1952.

————. *The Story of Electricity in Alabama Since the Turn of the Century*. Birmingham: Birmingham Publishing Co., 1952.

McMillian, Malcomb C. *The Land Called Alabama*. Austin, TX: Steck-Vaughn, 1975.

Mitchell, Sidney A. *S.Z. Mitchell and the Electrical Industry*. New York: Farrar, Strauss & Cudahy, 1960.

Murray, William M. Jr. *Thomas W. Martin: A Biography*. Birmingham: Southern Research Institute, 1978.

Noles, James L. Jr. *Alabama Power Company*. Charleston, SC: Arcadia Publishing, 2001.

Owen, Thomas McAdory. *History of Alabama and Dictionary of Alabama Biography*. 4 vols. Chicago: S.J. Clarke Publishing Co., 1921.

Owsley, Frank L. *Struggle for the Gulf Borderlands: The Creek War and the Battle of New Orleans*. Gainesville: University of Florida Press, 1981.

Pickett, Albert J. *History of Alabama and Incidentally of Georgia and Mississippi, from the Earliest Period*. Charleston, SC: Walker and James, 1851.

Reynolds, Hughes. *The Coosa River Valley from De Soto to Hydroelectric Power*. Cynthiana, KY: The Hobson Book Press, 1944.

Rivers of Alabama. Illustrated by Jack B. Hood. Art editor E.L. Klein. Huntsville, AL: Strode Publishers, 1968.

Rogers, William Warren, Robert David Ward, Leah Rawls Atkins, and Wayne Flynt. *Alabama: The History of a Deep South State*. Tuscaloosa: University of Alabama Press, 1994.

Schafer, Elizabeth D. "Saving the Good Earth: Mark Lovel Nichols, Soil Dynamics, and the Pioneering of Agricultural Engineering." Ph.D. dissertation. Auburn University, 1993.

Smith, Anita. *The Intimate Story of Lurleen Wallace: Her Crusade of Courage*. Edited by Ron Gibson. Montgomery, AL: Communications Unlimited, 1969.

Southerland, Henry D. Jr., and Jerry E. Brown. *The Federal Road through Georgia, the Creek Nation, and Alabama, 1806-1836*. Tuscaloosa: University of Alabama Press, 1989.

"Souvenir Issue of Lake Martin, the Largest Artificial Lake in the United States, and Martin Dam, Which Impounds This Great Body of Water Created by the Alabama Power Company." *Alabama Sportsman*, August-September 1926.

Swanton, John R. *Social Organization and Social Usages of the Indians of the Creek Confederacy*. Bureau of American Ethnology, Bulletin No. 42. Washington, D.C.: Government Printing Office, 1928. Reprint ed., New York: Johnson Reprint Co., 1970.

Tallapoosa Bicentennial Committee. *Tallapoosa County: A History*. Alexander City: Service Printing Co., 1976.

Thomas, Daniel H. *Fort Toulouse: The French Outpost at the Alabamas on the Coosa*. Introduction by Gregory Waselkov. Tuscaloosa: University of Alabama Press, 1989.

Toffel, Miriam Abigail, ed. *Women Who Made a Difference in Alabama*. Birmingham: The League of Women Voters of Alabama, 1995.

Waselkov, Gregory A., and Kathryn E. Holland Braund, eds. *William Bartram on the Southeastern Indians*. Lincoln: University of Nebraska Press, 1995.

Wells, Mary Ann. *Searching for Red Eagle: A Personal Journey into the Spirit World of Native America*. Jackson: University Press of Mississippi, 1998.

Williams, Jett, with Pamela Thomas. *Ain't Nothin' as Sweet as My Baby: The Story of Hank Williams' Lost Daughter*. New York: Harcourt Brace Jovanovich, 1990.

Wilson, Sandra S. *Some Early Pioneer Settlers of Tallapoosa County, Alabama*. Cullman, AL: Gregath Pub. Co., 1986.

Woodward, Thomas Simpson. *Woodward's Reminiscences of the Creek or Muskogee Indians*. Montgomery: Barett and Wimbish, 1859; reprint ed., Mobile: Southern University Press, 1965.

The WPA Guide to 1930s Alabama: Compiled by Workers of the Writers' Program of the Works Projects Administration in the State of Alabama. Introduction by Harvey H. Jackson III. Tuscaloosa: University of Alabama Press, 2000.

INDEX